"Sterry writes with comic brio . . . [He] honed a vibrant, outrageous writing style and turned out this studiously wild souvenir of a checkered past." — Janet Maslin, *The New York Times*

"This is a stunning book. Sterry's prose fizzes like a firework. As laconic as Dashiell Hammett, as viscerally hallucinogenic as Hunter S. Thompson. Sex, violence, drugs, love, hate, and great writing all within a single wrapper. What more could you possibly ask for?" — Maurice Newman, *Irish Times*

"Compulsively readable, visceral, and very funny. Rarely has the mentality of sex been so scrupulously observed and reproduced on paper. Granted, he had some amazingly bizarre experiences to draw upon; but as V. S. Pritchett observed, in memoirs you get no points for living, the art is all that counts—and David Henry Sterry clearly possesses the storyteller's art." — Phillip Lopate, author of *Portrait of My Body*

"Alternately sexy and terrifying, hysterical and weird, David Henry Sterry's *Chicken* is a hot walk on the wild side of Hollywood's fleshy underbelly. With lush prose and a flawless ear for the rhythms of the street, Sterry lays out a life lived on the edge in a coming-of-age classic that's colorful, riveting, and strangely beautiful. David Henry Sterry is the real thing." — Jerry Stahl, author of *Permanent Midnight*

"A beautiful book . . . a real work of literature . . . wonderfully written." —Vanessa Feltz, BBC

"Insightful and funny . . . great stories . . . captures Hollywood beautifully . . ." — Larry Mantle, *Air Talk*, National Public Radio

"Reading *Chicken* is like watching fireworks explode too closely: you shrink away, but just have to keep looking as the shrapnel descends around you. A breezy read, pleasingly free of self-pity . . . very funny."

— *The Observer*

"The overall effect is jarringly surreal, like an X-rated *Boogie Nights* narrated by a teenage Alice in Wonderland. Hollywood at its seamiest, a desperate city of smut and glitz. I read the book from cover to cover in one night, finally arriving at the black and white photo of the softly smiling former chicken turned memoirist."

— *Places Magazine*

"Reality porn for the sophisticated reader."

—Vicky Allan, *The Sunday Herald*

"Impossible to put down . . . Vulnerable, tough, innocent and wise . . . a great read."

— *Hallmemoirs*

"Sterry's an adventurer who happens to feel and think deeply. He's written a thoroughly absorbing story sensitively and with great compassion . . . A page-turner."

— Eileen Berdon, Erotica.com

"Love to see this book turned into a movie, Julianne Moore might like to play Sterry's mum . . ."

— Iain Sharp, *The Sunday Star-Times*, Auckland, New Zealand

Also by David Henry Sterry

The Essential Guide to Getting Your Book Published: How to Write It, Sell It and Market . . . Successfully (with Arielle Eckstut)

Hos, Hookers, Call Girls & Rent Boys: Professionals Writing on Life, Love, Money & Sex (with Richard Martin)

The Glorious World Cup: A Fanatic's Guide (with Alan Black)

Master of Ceremonies: A True Story of Love, Murder, Roller Skates & Chippendales

Putting Your Passion Into Print (with Arielle Eckstut)

Travis & Freddy's Adventures in Vegas (as Henry Johnson)

Satchel Sez: The World, Wit & Wisdom of Leroy Satchel Paige (with Arielle Eckstut)

Confessions of a Sex Maniac

Mort Morte (with illustrations by Alain Pilon)

CHICKEN

SELF-PORTRAIT OF A YOUNG MAN FOR RENT

10th ANNIVERSARY EDITION

DAVID HENRY STERRY

SOFT SKULL PRESS
AN IMPRINT OF COUNTERPOINT | BERKELEY

Library of Congress Cataloging-in-Publication Data

Sterry, David.
Chicken : self portrait of a young man for rent / David Henry Sterry;
foreword by Scott Buch.
pages cm
ISBN 978-1-59376-527-9 (alk. paper)
1. Sterry, David. 2. Male prostitutes—California—Los Angeles—Biography.
3. Male prostitution—California—Los Angeles.
4. Teenage prostitution—California—Los Angeles. I. Title.
HQ146.L7S74 2013
306.74'30979494--dc23
2013017907
Cover design by BriarMade
Interior design by Sabrina Plomitallo–González, Neuwirth & Associates

SOFT SKULL PRESS
An imprint of COUNTERPOINT
1919 Fifth Street
Berkeley, CA 94710
www.softskull.com

Printed in the United States of America
Distributed by Publishers Group West

10 9 8 7 6 5 4 3 2 1

Many names were changed to protect them and me.

This is dedicated to all the boys and girls who have been and continue to be victims of abuse at the hands of adults.

Ask for help.
Tell your story.

CHICKEN

Chick-en. noun, slang: a teenager who engages in indiscriminate sexual practices for money

Chicken Is 10 Years Old

Fifteen years ago somewhere in the neighborhood of 4 AM on a thick funk-filled Saturday morning, I find myself in the deep darkness of a dank cracksmoke-saturated Harlem house surrounded by a very attractive transsexual and a dozen disenfranchised Americans in various states of disrepair. A giant square-headed manbeast springs supernaturally fast at me with ice-fire eyes, his Python-biceped arm swinging a pipe at my head.

Dull thud of skull colliding with heavy metal pole reverberates down my spine and rattles the cage of my ribs. Luckily my people, as you will soon find out, are from the north of England, and have skulls so thick you can hammer in nails with them. Blood pours down my face like hot cherry fudge over a sundae. I don't even feel it. My skull is numb. I smile. I think that's what saves my life. They can't believe I'm standing there smiling with my head cracked open and a gusher of blood flowing freely down my face. As I slide bloody out of that Harlem crackhouse, I understand profoundly I have two choices. 1) Change. 2) Die.

Most suicides seem essentially selfish acts. Let's face it, unless you drown yourself tied to an anchor at sea, or get some animals to eat you, someone is going to have to clean up your mess. Often that appears to be half the point. So I'm not a suicide man, never have been. I can see clearly now looking back that I was frantically searching for someone to kill me.

I started writing this book fifteen years ago, when I escaped the Harlem franchise of the International House of Crack. Actually, the book I started writing is not the book you have in your hands. I had to write a whole different book first before I could write this one. It was a completely fictional novel filled with murdered fathers, violated children and Texas cheerleaders. Fifteen years ago I still couldn't tell my real story. I hadn't hit the bottom of the rock yet, and I still cared too much what everyone thought about me.

In fact, what you are reading has not, for me, been so much a book as a series of vehicles. Rickshaw, leaky canoe, 18-wheeler, broken-down mule, Spaceshuttle. It's taken me from the seedy groin of the Tenderloin to the finest opera houses in Europe; from dirty boulevards in the Bronx to the halls of the United States Department of Justice; from the haggis-filled streets of the Edinburgh Fringe Festival to the wall-to-wall dildoed halls of the Hustler Store on Sunset Strip; from the celebrity-engorged Groucho Club in London to pink smiling tulip cheeks at the Amsterdam University to diamond-hard eyes in gray granite faces at San Quentin prison.

Ten years ago when I finished the fictional version of my story, I had hit the bottom of the rock. The straw that broke my camel's hump was being dumped by a fiancée I DIDN'T EVEN LIKE. I showed my crazy manuscript about the murdered fathers, violated children, and Texas cheerleaders to everyone who would look at it. My ex-commercial acting agent Tina Jacobsen hooked me up with a book agent, her goddaughter. When I followed up a week after I sent the manuscript, the agent told me that she had already lost it. I took this as yet another sign that the universe despised me. But I re-sent my insane manuscript. One month later I called the agent. Asked her how her life was going. I was very nice to her. I didn't ask her about my manuscript. I found out later that because I was so nice, guilt forced my manuscript up about six inches from the bottom of a ten-foot pile, where it was suffocating under a thousand sweaty, hungry, bawling manuscripts. One month later: rinse and repeat. I was so sweet that my manuscript crept glacially up the pile a foot this time. I made variations on that phone call once a month for nine months. One human gestation period. We could have had a baby in the time it took this agent to read my book. At that point I had gone from an exquisite Craftsman home in the hills of Echo Park to Venice Beach, where you could satisfy all your crack needs by sticking your head out the window and proclaiming, "Yo!" Even though I had no actual plans to do so at the time, right before Thanksgiving I told her I was coming to New York for Christmas. My plan was to force her hand. It worked. She said if I came to New York she would take me to lunch and discuss my manuscript with me. I hung up the phone and booked a flight.

The agent did indeed take me to one of those fancy-ass Manhattany literary lunches to which agents take authors. She was warm witty winsome winning. Tres styly and chic without being pretentious. Smart deep brown eyes and a tight smoking-hot body. She told me smart things about my twisted manuscript. Said if I made the manuscript better, she'd try to sell it. The agent turned out to be one of those people who keeps getting more sexy the more they talk. She paid for lunch. Which I found very sexy. When I watched her and her tight smoking-hot ass walk away, I found her even sexier.

Having been recently dumped by a fiancée I DIDN'T EVEN LIKE, I had constructed a list of women in New York I'd like to be intimate with. The agent had, in fact, been number three. So the day after our lunch I started calling the lovely ladies on the List. The first two didn't pick up.

I left messages. I called the agent. She answered. I asked if she wanted to hang. She took me to a French restaurant for a late dinner. Near her apartment. After dinner she invited me back. We had one of those conversations where Einstein is proven right again, and two hours fly by like five minutes. Sitting in the sweetness of her couch she kinda smirked and said that every first novel was really about the writer's life. But this crazy book with all these murdered fathers and violated children and Texas cheerleaders can't be about your life, can it? She said it with a charming dollop of good-natured teasing that made me like her even more. But it was also clear that she was dead serious.

So I told her my story. I was finally ready. I had hit the bottom of the rock. I didn't care what she thought about me. That's what happens when you can go no lower. She told me that's the book I should write. So I did. Thus was born *Chicken*.

Two years six months and eleven days later, I married my agent on top of a mountain in California. Later that afternoon she fired me as her client.

Seven years two months and fourteen days later we had a baby together. She is sleeping peacefully upstairs.

It took me fifteen years to go from the crystal clarity one can only truly attain from a Harlem crackhouse at 4 AM, to the domestic bliss I find I am graced with as I thank the gods and goddesses that I am still alive ten years after I finished *Chicken*. Writing this book turned me into a different human being. I hope you, dearest reader, get to enjoy reading it as much as I enjoyed writing it.

1

THE TALL SEXY MAN

&

THE NUN

Children begin by loving their parents, after a time they judge them, rarely, if ever, do they forgive them. — Oscar Wilde

X X X

I WASN'T molested as a child. No one beat me with a coathanger. I was never burned by my evil babysitter's cigarette. I grew up in nice neighborhoods where kids played ball, swang on swings, and rode merry-go-rounds. Santa slid down my chimney, the Easter Bunny hid chocolate eggs in my yard, and the Tooth Fairy left a quarter under my pillow.

A rosy patina of relentless suburban niceness shimmers on the surface of my childhood: roses swimming gently in beds, summery-smelling freshly mown grass moaning, golden leaves floating down like autumnal coins; the taste of cold watery melon and the lick of a soft cloud of ice cream cone; toboggans and hot chocolate; Fourth of July fireworks and Tom Turkey Thanksgivings; Cream of Wheat mornings and Cat in the Hat nights.

You were happy where I grew up, and if you weren't, you had the decency not to mention it.

Into this brave New World came my mother and father, English immigrants from Newcastle, land of lily-skinned, thick-skulled, black-lunged,

Broon Ale-swigging Geordies, escaping a land as hard and cold as the coal you're not supposed to bring there.

My mom and dad became American citizens the instant they could, and we had a big party with sparklers twinkling atop a red-white-and-blue sugarlard-icing United States flag-covered cake.

My parents are in many ways embodiments of the American Dream. They came to this country with nothing but the clothes on their back, and after twenty years of hard work, sweat, and sacrifice, they were getting divorced, totally broke, and deep in therapy.

X X X

FRIDAY AFTERNOON in late Hollywood August, I'm seventeen-year-old freshmeat, just arrived to start my college career at Immaculate Heart College. Sister Liz, a tired nun in a wilted wimple, checks me into school. She reminds me of the Singing Nun from my childhood. Only she doesn't sing. I'm shocked. In exile at boarding school, I'd decided to go to college early. Only one place would take me without a high school diploma. Immaculate Heart College. Never dawned on my sixteen-year-old man-child idiot brain to ask for help with the application. Or, for that matter, to find out whether IHC had dorms. I didn't ask. And since it was decided I'd live with my Mom in LA, no housing arrangements had seemed necessary. But things change so quickly sometimes.

I have no place to sleep. I have $27 in the pocket of my nuthugging elephantbells. So I call my dad. He says he's having a cash-flow problem. I'm confused. My dad lives Jaguar large. He seems anxious to get me off the phone, and I can hear a woman who's definitely not my mom laughing and carrying on in the background.

"Whatever—" I manage to mumble.

Then I hang up.

I consider calling my mom. I quickly reject the idea. The fact that her young lover has, in my mind, replaced me in her life is just too much bad medicine to swallow.

I ask Sister Liz if they have a place for me to crash. She sighs heavy as she tells me they're not insured for student crashing. She suggests in no uncertain terms that perhaps it would've been a good idea if I had, you know, called ahead and made arrangements.

"Whatever—" I manage to mumble again.

I store my bags. I walk out of Immaculate Heart College, seventeen, no place to sleep, $27 to my name, and an angry beehive in my skull.

The weight of it sinks me to the curb, my head coming to rest in my hands. Six months ago I was guzzling rotgut and smoking angel wings at boarding school. Now my American Dream family's exploded like a landmine in a bomb shelter, and the shrapnel is flying thick and fast all around me.

IHC sits high atop a hill looking down on Hollywood, its superstar billboards looming over thick boulevards crammed with large cars. As a sweet breeze blows, the Lost Angel Siren sings her beautiful melody to me, and I'm sucked toward that voice no man can resist.

Next thing I know I'm strolling down the hill into Tinsel Town, swallowing my pain like a poison-pea pellet, and replacing it with what I intend to be a peacocky strut. I'm working hard to perfect my strut.

My hair is brown, thick and deep, my legs are thick muscles wrapped up tight in nuthugging elephantbells. I'm packing long feet and big hands, a too-tight T with a Rolling Stones tongue licking the world, and red hightops. One green sock, one blue sock.

I have no idea where I'm going, or what I'm doing, but as I bust my strut up the gut of Hollywood and float over the sidewalkstars, I feel for no reason that it is a good day to be alive, with these palm trees waving at me and this afternoon sun bathing on my face in this new place, my past back there, and my future right in front of me on the Boulevard of Dreams.

I walk all the way up Hollywood Boulevard to Grauman's Chinese Theater: past touristas snapping shots; wannabe starlets sparkling by in miniskirts with headshots in their hands and stardust in their eyes; rowdy cowboys drinking with drunken Indians; black businessmen bustling by brisk in crisp suits; ladies who do not lunch with nylons rolled up below the knee pushing shopping carts full of everything they own; Mustangs rubbing up against muscular Mercedes and Hell's Angel hogs.

It's a sick twisted Wonderland, and I am Alice.

X X X

MY MOM was an emotional woman who cried at the drop of a pin. At the drop of a hat. At the drop of a hatpin. Calm ivory skin, sturdy oak hair, a grand laugh, and smart dark eyes full of love. She could make a wild wailing hard-baked baby coo with the soothe of her touch. Her father, a professional athlete and amateur pedophile, was an olive-hued man of black silences, eyes, and hair.

My dad was a chemist and mathematician, distant, intellectual, wracked with silence masked by snappy patter. He was one of the fair, freckled folk of the North of England. Not tall, with a bony nose, he was spindly, nimble, quick, and tricky. Dad had a big brain. He was the first in his family to go to college, unheard of for a coal miner's son. And that man could work. Work, work, work. He was wound Newcastle-coal tight to begin with, and every minute he worked he seemed to get a little tighter. But at a time when being a Provider was paramount, he was a para-mount Provider. My dad had love in his heart, he just had no idea how to get it out.

His brain and her heart took my mom and dad from the oothooses and broon ale of an English pit village, to the heart of America, with a beautiful five-bedroom Spanish-style craftsman, complete with a swimming pool, servants' quarters, and a fountain spewing pompously in the front yard.

X X X

MARILYN MONROE'S handprints are staring at me. I'm standing in front of Grauman's, smack dab in the middle of this Hollywood Friday night.

"Marilyn . . . now there was a woman."

A tall black man stares at me. He's wearing a black shirt that says SEXY in silver sparkly letters. He's the first person I talk to in LA who's not a nun.

"Yeah . . . Marilyn . . ." I have no idea what I'm talking about.

"My old lady say she was fat, but I like a woman with an ass on her," drawls the tall black man.

"Yeah, a woman's gotta have an ass . . . on her." I'm just trying to keep up.

"Now Marilyn, she was a movie star. Not like these bitches today. No style. Skanky, bony-assed bitches . . ."

The tall black sexy man starts walking. I walk with him. Seems like the thing to do.

"Where you from?" he asks.

I don't know how to answer this question. I'm not from anywhere right now, and the panic punches me in the nuts. Then I remember reading in a magazine that when you feel anxious or irritated, all you have to do is change the record in your head. Replace the bad thoughts with good thoughts. So that's what I do. I change the record. I'm in Hollywood, it's packed with exciting people from all over the world, and I'm one of them.

"I said, 'Where you from?'" the sexy man repeats.

"All over . . ." I'm trying so hard to be Whatever.

"I been there," he says. "Hell, I've been there and back."

I laugh, he laughs, then all of a sudden we're laughing together.

"Where you live?" he asks.

"Around . . ." I attempt a world weary smile, but it doesn't work.

"Hey, you hungry? Wanna steak?" asks the SEXY man.

Steak. Yes. Good. Steak. That's the best idea I've heard in a donkey's age, as my mom used to say.

He walks, I walk, then all of a sudden we're walking together, talking about thisandthat, nothing really, just easy talk. We wander off Hollywood Boulevard onto a side street and into a stucco apartment building that at one time had almost certainly been white but is now a beigy grey.

He leads me through a dust bowl of a lobby that smells of bad booze, soiled cigarettes, and stale cats; up a staircase where boogeymen peek out from the darkunder; and down a hallway where a rotten orange of a bloodstained carpet crawls.

He opens a door, and starts to lead me into a dark apartment.

If this was a movie, I would've yelled at the screen—

"Don't go in that door!"

But this is not a movie, so I waltz right in without blinking or batting an eye or a lash. I'm really looking forward to my steak.

SEXY flips on a dim little light, and a poster of a Negrita with thigh-high boots, hothothotpants, a mushroomcloud Afro, and a mouth that promises untold excitement stares at me. "Foxy Chocolate" is the title, I think, although I can't be sure.

I sit on a sad overripe couch. It's snowing inside the television. The tall man in the shirt that says SEXY disappears into the kitchen. I should really call my dad. I look around. There are corpses of ancient alumi-num foil frozen dinners, cold old chicken bones, and industrial-size malt liquor cans standing like headstones over the graves of dead beers. But no phone. I try to concentrate on the show behind the snow, where excited people are winning something from a silvertongued devil in a shiny suit, whipping frenzy into a salivating studio audience.

SEXY appears with two pink steaks on two green plates.

Just two pink steaks on two green plates.

"Hunger is the best sauce," my mom used to say.

And I am hung-a-ry.

The smell invades me and my carnivore growls, salivary glands pumping a rich river of digestive fluids down my throat, as I rip into the meat of it, teeth sinking in warm flesh, bloody juice flooding my tongue, hot flesh sliding down my gullet.

Before I know it, only the green plate is left.

My eyelids suddenly feel like safes being thrown from a tall building. I haven't slept much lately.

"Wanna crash?" his tall sexy baritone slides over me like a chocolate mousse smoothie.

Crash. Yes. Crash. Good idea. He leads me into his black bedroom. I'm asleep on my feet, shuffling toward the bed that waits to embrace me. I remove my shoes, and put them at the foot of a falling-apart chair that looks like my Uncle Ronnie home from a heavy night boozing. An old coat in the corner resembles a large slouching rodent. A lizard shoe flicks its tongue at me. The steak is warm and yummy, resting like a hamster in the tummy of a snake as I curl into the skank of the mattress.

I'm asleep.

X X X

I'M EXILED to the Elba of boarding school for my sins when I'm sixteen. I don't want to be expelled from my family, but no matter how much kick I put in my scream, my mom and dad ignore me. So I suck it up, pack up my troubles, and take it like a man.

Whatever.

As a result, I'm a little unclear exactly what happened late back in Dallas, but this much I have gathered:

1) My mom moves her friend into my recently vacated room.

2) One afternoon my dad comes home from his explosives plant and discovers my mother—his wife—in his bed with her new best friend.

3) All hell breaks loose.

X X X

RED ROCKETS rip into me, blasting a bolt of agony up my buggered guts, splitting my heart and burying shafts of pain in my brain. I've severed ligaments, snapped ribs, shattered toes, cracked a head, and broken a nose, but I've never felt pain like that.

I can't see anything. Can't hear anything. Can't smell anything. Can't touch anything. Can't taste anything.

All there is is pain.

I try to yank away, but I can't move. I don't know how he did it, but the tall sexy man has gotten inside me, impossibly huge and violent, and he has me pinned, his chest pressed into my back, right arm underneath me, holding my shoulder, hot breath stenching my neck, growling into my ear like a feeding beast, punishing me with the flame of his rage, tearing a hole in me.

Smell's the first sense to return, as the funk of the sour-beer old moldy body-fluid mattress fills my face.

Sound's next. He's calling me a PUNK and a BITCH and a FAGGOT as he rapes me, tearing a hole in my soul.

Everything slowmotions now. I ram my right arm up fast as I can, the hard bone of elbow driving into the soft cartilage of his Adam's apple, a sucking pain sound jolting out of him as he yanks back, breath spasming asthmatically.

Whipping him out of me, I'm suddenly blessedly empty.

I move fast now, all animal instinct, while he wheezes from the bed, I grab my shoes, shoot through the bedroom, stumble, stub my toe on the couch.

I hear my brain say, "Stubbed toe on couch." But there's no pain. I slam open the door, flash down the hall, leap three steps at a time, fly the lobby onto the street, and hit the hot pavement running fast as I can.

Slowing slightly in the cool latenight earlymorning air, I slip into my red hightops. I do not stop to tie them.

As I speedwalk onto Hollywood Boulevard, Saturday morning's

moving in on Friday night, and the vampires are scurrying in before the first ray of dawn turns them to dust. Smells like an ashtray. Streetlights aren't off yet, and the dark chill clings still as night tries desperately not to give up the ghost.

I jam past the hungry hookers and the horny johns who don't have enough money, the smackdaddies and the boozebabies, the clodhoppers and the pillpoppers.

Plodding along over and under the fading stars, the adrenaline anaesthetic begins to wear off and the pain creeps in, starting at the tip of the bottom, and pulsating an ache that shoots all the way up through me.

A thick cloud of tears appears. Everything hurts. I deserve it. But I won't cry. I don't understand how tears work yet.

Oh God, I'm so tired. I grimace, limping gingerly, trying not to breathe too much, head down shuffling, stargazing to keep from dropping off the face of the earth.

I can barely keep putting one foot in front of the other. But the fear that SEXY is following spreads like a brush fire through my ass and keeps me moving at a brisk clip.

I feel a wet between my legs. I reach inside my pants. Warm thick liquid pools. I pull out my hand. It's red with my blood.

I reach into my pocket. My $27 is gone.

2

THE HOLY POULTRY GRAIL

My bucket's got a hole in it. — Hank Williams

X X X

HUNGRY.

Saturday morning is waking up, shops opening their mouths and yawning, seers of sights emerging from cheap hotels on their way to big American breakfasts.

Hungry.

Bloody and nasty, I wander like a moving violation down Hollywood Boulevard, the sun slowly exposing herself, as the smells of eggs, bacon, and pancakes force a hollow rumble in my stomach that distracts me from the unholy pain in my ass.

As pink peeks out from under the horizon I pass Hollywood Fried Chicken. I'm so tired I can't take another step, so I lean like a broken soldier into the shadow of a dumpster.

Soon as I stop, the tears are there again, close enough to drink.

A greasy chicken perfume croons from inside the dumpster, and when I peer in I spot an almost full container of almost uneaten chicken. I reach into the dumpster, but even on tiptoes I can't quite grab the bucket. The hunger hoists me up, and before I know it I'm in the dumpster, trash swallowing my red hightops, air thick with rotted coleslaw and rancid meat. As orange joins pink around the rim of Hollywood, I can't tell where the garbage ends and I begin. But there's no turning back. I can see clearly now that my future depends on reaching this holy poultry grail.

I wade through skanky refuse. I reach down, grab that bucket of chicken, and hold it over my head like I just won a gold medal in Olympic dumpster hunting.

It's full of legs and thighs. No wings. Just legs and thighs. I take this as a good sign.

I can feel someone watching me. I look up. The sun blinds me with its first fullfaced appearance of the day, and there is the silhouette of the tall black man in the shirt that says SEXY.

I clench unconsciously and a mad stab of pain sears me. I sink to my knees in stinking filth, clinging to my chicken. Slowly he moves toward me, and my blood roars, drowning out all the Hollywood morning noise.

I'm going to die in this dumpster. I know it now. A deep peace sweeps through me. Death can't possibly be any worse than this, I think, as SEXY steps forward to kill me.

X X X

MY FATHER later told me he first suspected something was hinky with my mom when he found a book in a bag she packed for a trip with her new friend who'd moved into my vacated room.

The book was called *A Woman's Orgasm*, or *Women and Their Orgasms*, or *Orgasms and Women*. Something like that.

I don't think my father was aware at the time that a woman could actually have an orgasm, but even he knew this was not a good sign for the marriage.

X X X

SEXY STEPS forward, and leans on the dumpster. I can see him clearly for the first time now. It's not SEXY. It's someone else. A new black man. And he's small, not tall. He's smiling. At me. With deep, teasing coffee eyes—

"Whatchew doin' boy?"

This is my problem in a nutshell. I have no idea what I'm doing. But his voice is smooth, loose, and soothing, like a lily pad floating in a warm Savannah pond. It makes everything unclench.

"You lookin' to git you some chickin?"

I swear to God he's flirting with me. I squeam. Fool me once I'm an idiot. Fool me twice I'm twice as big an idiot. I want to say something. I need to say something. But my father's jaw locks around my mouth, and it will not open.

"Git out the dumpster, boy, Ah'll give you some chickin." He's all mint julep Old South Charm School charm.

I'm paralyzed, raw and sore, a wounded freak in a trash cage. God seems to be reaching his hand out to me. But what would God be doing in Hollywood? And what if it's not God at all? What if it's the Devil? Having just met the Devil, I'm terrified of the prospect of a return engagement.

"Come on boy, git out the dumpstah . . ."

The small sexy man clucks like a hen den mother.

Dazed and confused, I put down the chicken, hop out of the dumpster, and brush off some scum.

"Eh toi son, what you doin' loikin' 'round this nasty ol' dumpster, like some skinny-asks flea on a bony-butt dog? For real, whatchew doin' in there, boy?" Big brown doe-boy eyes size me up. "You in trouble? You need you a job?"

A job. Yes. A job. That's what I need. That's exactly what I need. Or is this small black sexy man just jacking with me so he can crack me open like a ripe melon?

"What kind of job?" I say, full of need and please.

"Fryin' chickin, boy," he cracks wise, "whatchew think? You do know this is a fried chicken restaurant don't you? I swear to God, you ain't got the sense God gave a midget-brained monkey. And what kind of ways dat to talk? You should be saying, 'Thank you Sunny, for saving my ass, you're going straight to heaven, Sunny.' That's what you should be said. Used here boy, which would you rather be: having a job or you can make you some real money? Or are loikin' round dis nasty ol' dumpster like a choichmouse in a room full of three-bald cats?"

When he puts it like that, seems pretty obvious.

"Uh, a job . . ."

My new best friend walks toward the back door of Hollywood Fried Chicken.

I follow three or four feet behind, wary, wounded, and feral. He takes out an oversized key ring, opens one lock, then another, then the big black back door. Then he enters.

I hover like my own ghost just outside the doorway, smelling that deep comforting chicken fry smell. He punches some numbers into a small box on the wall. If the guy has the keys and knows how to turn off the alarm, he's gotta be the manager. Right?

"Boy, don't jest stand there, come awn in."

He holds out an apron. I have to enter to take it. I enter. I take it. I put it on. Feels good to belong to something.

I have no idea what a wonderful joke the gods are playing on me. Torn apart and lost in a dumpster, at the lowest moment in my young life, I'm brought face to face with the man who'll teach me all about chicken.

How to fry one. How to be one.

X X X

CUCKOLDED BY his goodwife, my dad's response is to buy her and her new lover a brand new Pinto, a car manufactured by the Ford Motor Company.

Pintos were soon recalled by Ford. Something about their gas tanks having a nasty habit of exploding. In addition, the doors were too heavy, so after a while the weight of them, combined with the force of gravity, made them fall quite off.

So when my mom eased out of the driveway in Dallas with her kids (minus me), and her young lover, headed for the rest of her new life, she was doing so in a time bomb with the doors falling off.

X X X

FOUR MINUTES.

That's how long it takes me to learn everything there is to know about the industrial frying of chicken.

1) Soak chicken bits in foul yellowish liquid.

2) Dump into batter.

3) Shake until fully glommed.

4) Dump batter-glommed chicken bits into industrial-strength boiling oil-filled inferno fryer.

5) Set dials.

6) Lock and load fryer.

7) When buzzer buzzes dump deeply fried chicken bits onto tray and slide under megamagma heat lamps.

Sunny explains all this to me very slowly, like I'm a glue sniffer who just smoked angel dust. He begins going over the whole thing again, but stops and stares when he sees I'm already doing it.

In Hueytown, Alabama, when something's slightly off, people say: "Nigger in the woodshed."

Several times that day I catch Sunny scrutinizing me like a bug under a microscope. He starts to say something, then backs off chuckling. This is what it looks like he's thinking: "Nigger in the woodshed."

Having a task is a great distraction from the searing sensation in my shredded ass, the Where am I gonna live? Where is my next meal coming from? Why does everyone hate me? Questions.

I fry thousands of chickens and eat several hundred. The night shift guy doesn't show, so I work a double, and by ten o'clock closing time I feel a mutant poultry experiment gone wrong, ready to run away with the carnival and become a geek: "Step right up and see Chicken Boy! He's half-human, half-extra crispy fried chicken. Ladies and gentleman, he's gonna bite his own head off!"

Even though my hair is turning into feathers, my feet into claws, my nose a beak, and I have no lips, I feel good. For the first time in a long time, I've been given a challenge to rise to. And I have risen.

After I've polished the deep fryers to within an inch of their lives, Sunny comes over, puts his arm around me like the black brother I never had, and smiles.

"You done good t'day, boy."

I have no home, no money, and I smell really bad, but when Sunny says I done good, my heart soars like the eagle.

"Where you stayin' tonight?" drawls Sunny.

Oh shit. Sleep. Bed. Roof over head. Right. In all the excitement I've forgotten: yet another crucial top level executive decision faces me.

As he looks at me I quickly review my options:

A) Wander the Hollywood streets all night and hope I don't get mutilated again.

B) Find someone on the streets to take me in for the night then bash my head and trash my ass.

C) I have absolutely no idea.

I'm forced to admit that both short and long term prospects do not look good.

"You ain't gotchoo no place to stay tonight, do ya boy?" Sunny's like the lawyer who knows the answer before he asks the question.

"No, no, no ... I'm not, you know ... see, uh, I gotta little situation, and ... it's not really ... uh ..."

The sentence gets off to a very bad start and never really recovers.

"Yeah, Ah got the picha ..." Sunny nods. "You know what yo' problem is?"

"No ..." I really want to know what my problem is.

"You too smart for ya own damn good," Sunny laughs. "You wanna crash to mah pad, that's cool ..." slides out of him real easy.

I know that as far as offers go, that's as good as it's gonna get on this chicken-filled night. Waiting in the parking lot with my funked-up ass for Sunny to take me Godknowswhere and do Godknowswhat to me, I almost bolt into the starry Hollywood night. But where will I go? What will I do? My mom? Fat chance. She doesn't want me around. Bitch. Life's a bitch. I'm a bitch.

Change the record. Now.

I tail Sunny to his car, walking on cat's paws. He unearths his keys. They have a rabbit's foot on them. I breathe. Can someone with a rabbit's foot be truly evil?

Moby Dick is the name I give Sunny's car. It's a cross between a tank, a dictator's limo, and a pre-historic albino rhino. It's brand new, and big enough to house a family of refugees. Gold spokes gold bumpers gold grill. The gear shift knob looks like a giant golden Cyclops testicle. It is a Conquistador's wet dream.

Inside Sunny's combination automobile/lifestyle/moveable feast, it's like I'm on a crazy movie set where everything's way too big so the actors look teenytiny. Barry White throbs on the wraparound stereo with his huge deep growly sexmusic. I swear it's like Barry's sweating and moaning in the car with us.

Then it hits me: how the hell can a guy who's manager of Hollywood Fried God Damn Chicken afford wheels like this?

Nigger in the woodshed.

But as soon as I focus on this paradox, a picture of my tall sexy violator man flashes in my ass, and I bite my cuticle, ripping into the flesh with my teeth, pulling off a chunk of skin, my finger bleeding.

Sunny's apartment complex sits like a grey sore on the scruffy neck of Hollywood. All it needs is a searchlight and some German shepherds to make the Stalag 17 effect complete. Sunny and I disembark from the belly of his great whale into the bowels of the building. He walks me through the concrete courtyard past the grungy fungi-filled pool, complete with its own water troll lurking in the boggy depths.

3D reads the door that Sunny throws open.

Perfect. Where else would Sunny live?

Suddenly I'm all clammy and slabby and crappy, and the ache of my pain screams: "Don't walk in 3D!"

Then I have a moment of clarity. I've got no money, no place to sleep, and I don't think I can stay awake all night.

I walk in 3D.

A fluorescent orange couch crouches in the middle of the room, creaking like a rusty whore when Sunny plops down on it. I lower myself into a giant once-green once-overstuffed chair. It's like sitting on an anorexic greyhound. I wonder why Sunny doesn't put plumbing and a bed in Moby Dick and live in there.

Sunny asks me if I want anything, says he's got some chicken wings in the icebox.

"If you make me look at one more piece of chicken today, I will have no choice but to kill you." I'm tired enough to actually be my real self for a second, and Sunny laughs. I breathe again.

Then he gets up and walks out of the room, leaving me alone with my worst enemy.

Myself.

Suddenly the savages creep in from the closets, crawl out from under the rug, and sneak in from the bathroom whispering how Sunny's gonna tie me up and make me squeal like a pig. I see me naked, my dead head resting on a pillow of my own blood.

X   X   X

I'M DUE to fly to Hollywood to attend Immaculate Heart College in a couple of weeks, to live with my brother, my sisters, my mother, and her new young lover, so I call my mom to make pickup arrangements.

She sounds off balance. Tells me she's decided to stay up in Oregon because its so nice there. And since I'm already enrolled in college, and tuition is paid, I should just go to Immaculate Heart in Hollywood.

The beige phone is cold and hard in my hand as my heart sinks to the rug that's been pulled out from under me.

Suddenly there's no air in my lungs.

X   X   X

SUNNY EMERGES in a long shiny teal satin boxing robe, and when he sinks into the loudly complaining orange couch, he looks like a twisted little Howard Johnson's.

He carries a two-foot hollow cylindrical plastic tube, three-quarters full of water, with tubes sticking out of it, and a small bowl from a pipe attached to the side. He pulls a baggie from his imitation wood end table, removes some green leafy substance, stuffs it snugly into the pipe bowl, and lights it, while holding one finger over a hole in the back of the cylinder. He tokes it and stokes it, and when the cylinder fills thick with smoke, Sunny removes his finger from the hole, and when he sucks hard, the smoke shoots Old Faithful style into his mouth, disappears into him.

Then he leans back and smacks his lips, like he's savoring a fine wine, and holds his breath for a very very very very very long time, then slowly lets the smoke roll out like tumbling dice, smiling contentedly as he passes me the smoking bazooka.

I take my suck, the smoke creeps into the cylinder, and when I uncover the hole and pull in, it sledgehammers into me. It expands inside me, like someone's blowing up a balloon inside my lungs, and when I let it out I'm totally relaxed and wildly invigorated, waterfalls, popsicles, and plasticine porters with looking glass ties floating right before my eyes, which go to half-mast as if the president has died inside my head. And with no effort at all a huge goofy grin blooms across my face.

"Why don't you come over here, boy, Ah got somethin' for your ass . . ." drawls Sunny.

So here it is. I knew it was coming, and now it's here. He's gonna try to do me.

"Okay, look . . ." I assume the chest-puffed fist-clenched bull-monkey position. "I appreciate the job and, you know . . . everything, but . . . if you try to . . . you know . . . I'm gonna have to . . . mess you up . . . good . . ."

Even as it's coming out I know my attempt at badness is an extremely limp biscuit. I'm half a second from making a mad dash for the door when Sunny busts out laughing.

"Ah hope to God you don't try that mess in public, cuz that's a good way to git yourself bitchslapped, son." Sunny howls, one of those wake-up-the-neighbors bellylaughs that shakes a foundation, and of course that makes me laugh, and then the both of us are cackling like a couple of hyenas on laughing gas, and it feels like warm waves of sunshine rippling in an Indian summer afternoon.

Sunny tells me he can fellate me better than any woman ever could. And the way he says it, it seems like it's probably true. He tells me he loves boys, has loved boys since he was a boy himself. Countless women have tried to convert him. They always tell him he just never met the right girl. But he likes boys. Always has. Always will. "Unless Ah git hit by lightnin', or Jesus saves my ass, and don't think he ain't tried."

I tell Sunny I don't want him to fellate me. I ask him if I can stay there without the fellatio. He says I can. I ask him if he's gonna try fellating me while I'm asleep. He asks me if I want him fellating me while I'm asleep. I assure him that I don't. He tells me if that's the case, there will be no fellatio.

Into the night I lie with one eye open on the bony carcass of his sofa, listening for the sound of Sunny coming to splay me open as I doze in fits and starts.

When I wake up in the morning, panic swarms. Where am I? Boarding school? No. My dad's house in Dallas? My mom and her young lover's house? No. No. Desperately I try reviving my brain while I figure out my longitude and latitude.

A snore roars from the bedroom. Snore. Sunny. I'm at Sunny's. He hasn't molested me. My ass sighs. I breathe. Not easy. But at least I breathe.

For the time being.

X X X

HOLDING THE phone I want to pick one of the millions of thoughts racing through my brain in the single second my mother tells me she does not want me.

"Can't I come up and live with you? Please help me! Whataboutmewhataboutmewhataboutme?"

But I can't ask.

"Whatever—" I manage to mumble. It's becoming my dysfunctional mantra.

I hang up.

The hole in my bucket gets a little bigger.

X X X

EXISTENTIALISM, HUMANITIES, poetry, math for poets. These are the classes at Immaculate Heart College. A couple of fellow IHC dudes let me rent their living room, and I convert it into my boudoir by making walls out of some nasty roadkill carpet I find on the street.

Turns out IHC's run by radical nuns. I like the nuns. Even though they're Catholic and I'm not, they seem to hate the church almost as much as I do. Urban legend has it that when Patty Hearst was on the lam, the nuns took her in at Immaculate Heart College. Later they'll get ex-comunicated, or made redundant, or whatever it's called when the Pope kicks an order of nuns out of his church.

I fry approximately 1,000,000,000 chickens, spattered with boiling oil, perpetually covered with a thick layer of chicken stank that will not wash off. And since it's free, I gorge extra-crispy by the stomachful. I don't talk to my mom. I want to, but there's a collection of stumps where I've been clearcut from her forest. I try to talk to my father. He seems uninterested. So I pretend I'm uninterested. I'm too lost in the Sea of Silence to tell anybody about my ass.

Sunny's much more loving to me than my mom or my dad. Of course, he does want to have sex with me. And in fairness to my folks, my dad's just been dumped for a lesbian and my mom's just been made a social outcast for becoming one.

I've been working at Hollywood Fried Chicken a few weeks now. It's closing time. I've shined the deep fryers so I can see myself in them. I don't like the way I look. Sunny walks over and stares right into me for a long time. Makes me feel uncomfortable, and I'm already greasy and queasy from all that extra crispy I've fried and eaten.

I'm tired of eating extra crispy. I'm tired of being broke. I'm tired of having a pain in my ass.

I'm tired.

"You ready, boy?" asks Sunny.

"Ready for what?" I ask.

"Real Money," Sunny smiles.

That week I deepfried about a billion chickens. I made seventy-eight dollars after taxes. That's chicken scratch. In fact, the more I think about it, the more I know I'm ready for some Real Money.

Sunny tells me he's got rich, generous, horny friends. These friends, he explains, will pay good money to party with a boy like me. I can make the Real Money and have all the pussy I can shake a stick at. Not that I'm anxious to shake a stick at any pussy, but he certainly got my attention.

I started having sex when I was thirteen, and I took to it like a well-watered carrot in fertile earth. Already, I'm fluent in Sex. I take direction well. I love making women feel good, and I've learned the importance of a slow hand, a sweet mouth, and paying attention.

I hear destiny calling my name.

3

MY HYMEN

&

A WEDGWOOD EGG

If love is the answer, could you rephrase the question? — Lily Tomlin

X X X

THE PALMTREE streets that line the colossal estates make me feel right
at home: an exiled caterpillar reborn a badboy butterfly. I'm rich
and big in this world, an All-American success, rising from dumpster
fisher to humpster of the rich and famous in the time it takes to split
a second.

I park my bike down the street as instructed, and steal, nerves jangling,
guts rumbling, through the mansion's reargate, a backdoor boy sliding in
past the fountain sculpture of a fat angel, and into the former servants'
quarters where my Frannie waits to pop my professional cherry.

Like some flaming 'enry 'iggins Sunny schooled me on The Rules:

1) Don't be late.

2) Don't rip anybody off.

3) Don't do drugs.

4) Be clean.

5) Say as little as possible.

6) When in doubt say even less.

7) The customer's always right.

8) If something seems weird it probably is.

And the three most important rules of the world of industrial sex:

1) Get the money up front!

2) GET THE MONEY UP FRONT!

3) GET THE MONEY UP FRONT!

Sunny made me look him in the eyes and repeat:

"GET THE MONEY UP FRONT!"

He calls the customers tricks. It's my job to trick them.

Soon thereafter Sunny, who's now my boss/employment coun-
selor/father confessor/fairy godmother/pimp, sends me off on my
date with fate.

X X X

MARIE, A senior girl, is teaching me about the hypnotic power of cunnilingus when I'm fifteen. I'm in love with Gina, my sweet-hearted girlfriend
who's finally letting me go both down on and into her. I'm also friends
with Sheila, a wrong-side-of-the-tracks girl who heaps massive affection
on me if I'm good to her, which is easy cuz she's funny smart and nice.
I know if the girls find out about each other, the whole thing'll collapse.
So I make sure they don't. I like the secret life. It makes the sex more
exciting. The silence is familial and familiar.

Very soon the synapses that fire like copulation cannons during forni-
cation become synonymous with love. Replace happiness with pleasure.
I couldn't feel so I tried to touch. The whole thing is great training for
being a chicken.

X X X

I TRAMP up Frannie's stairs in my testicle-nuthugging elephantbells and painted-on GRUNT T, hoping for the best and expecting the worst. There's way too much desperation in my strut.

I tremor as I enter Frannie's too-blue bedroom with the four-poster bed, stuffy flowerprint couch, and print of what I now realize was Monet's *Water Lilies*, like a scared little school boy sent to do a man's job. Will I be a loverstudguy or a houseboy?

Frannie's mophandle, pipecleaner, stickfigure thin. Roasted chestnut hair cut in a stylish post-pageboy. Huge ruby ringed by diamonds on her long spindle of a finger. Kindling twig arms. Perfectly manicured nails the same color as the red wine she imbibes in thin persistent sips. Designer sweatpants and overpriced sweatshirt that swallow her whole. Tony sunglasses resting on bony sandstone cheekbones. Exotic sandals engulfing emaciated x-ray toes.

Frannie's neither the nightmare nor the wet dream. She's just Frannie, perched like an anorexic bird in the plumage of her couch, motioning to the Louis Quatorze dressing table with the inlaid mirror where a crisp new hundred-dollar bill luxuriates. My heart skips rope. I try to look Bondcalmsuave as I pick it and pocket it. It feels good hot on my thigh, a prize for the desire I arouse, cold hard cash evidence that I'm somebody cuz somebody wants to pay to have sex with me.

Frannie seems to be going through all the motions of being a rich woman, but there's something not quite all there about Frannie. She doesn't say much. She wants me to talk. She'll hint later in our relationship that something happened to her. Something horrible and weird. Something that would make anyone not quite all there.

It's a vacancy I will grow very familiar with in the world of industrial sex.

As Frannie listens to me I wonder why on earth this pretty rich lady would hire a seventeen-year-old-boy whore. Months later I'll ask her about the horrible weird thing she hinted at, trying to get my mind around the whole thing. She'll look at me sharply and snap—"I don't pay you for that!" I'll feel like dirty vermin. But I'll be a professional. I'll assassinate the part of myself that cares.

Whatever.

X X X

OUR FAUX-WOODPANELED stationwagon is toodling through the suburbs. My mom's driving. I'm fifteen, riding shotgun. We're having a pleasant chat, about nothing really, thisandthat, just easy talk. My mother's been through quite a bit of liberation by now. Her consciousness has left the kitchen and is on its way up the stairs to the master bedroom. What it will do there is anyone's guess.

She and I are transitioning from son-caretaker/mother-wife, to real friends.

I don't know exactly how we got here, but we're talking about girls I've had sex with. Mom's curious, I can tell. She wants to know if I like it. I tell her I like it very much. I ask her if she likes it. She phumphs.

But the can of worms is open. I can see the worms wiggling around inside the can, and I'm not about to pass up this opportunity to get them out and play with them.

X X X

VAGINAS, CLITORI, breasts, legs, how they smell, what noises they make, how they like it: spare no detail, and use all the naughty words. That's what Frannie wants to know about all the girls I've been with. As a manchild ho whose mom's a brand-new lesbian, it's my theory that Frannie really wants to be with a woman. But I'm not about to tell her that. Don't want to queer a good thing.

Frannie instructs me to take my clothes off. Many many many times in my chicken career, women will want me naked while they're fully clothed. Some people don't like being naked. I do. Another example of how the job is a good match for my skill set.

I catch myself in the mirror, seventeen-year-old hardbody belly, pitprop legs, zero body fat, and huge hands, I'm seduced by the glitter of my own flesh.

On the first day of my rookie season, Frannie gives me excruciatingly explicit directions in her droll monotone, detailing exactly what she wants me to do and how she wants me to do it. I'm ready. I was born for this work. I want to be good so bad I can taste it.

Frannie slips her slippers off, hunkers undercover, then wiggles out of her pants. Never removes her sweatshirt. She lies on her back, eyes clamped, legs closed tight, in the corpse position.

I crawl in under from the bottom of the bed, a manchildbeast creeping between her legs, the silence like a sweet kissing cousin. Then I pleasure her as I love myself in the old fashioned way.

Just as she ordered, to the letter.

I'm playing the part of a hundred-dollar-an-hour loverstudguy. Only after a while I'm not playing the character—I am the character. Feels good to pleasure the mysterious and rich Frannie. I do it for a very long time, whispering underbreath what a sexynaughtyfilthybaby she is.

As per her request.

✗ ✗ ✗

"DO YOU and dad ever do oral sex?" I ask.

"Oh no . . . no, no . . ." my mom shakes her head.

"So, you've never done sixty nine?" I ask.

She looks at me as if I'd said, "How many brillig did the flipper orangutan?"

"Do you even know what sixty-nine is?" I ask.

"No, not really," says my mom.

My mom's never been afraid to say she doesn't know, and I love that about her.

"Simultaneous oral stimulation of the genitals."

I read that somewhere.

I can see my mom putting it all together in her head like a mathematical equation. Simultaneous + Oral + Stimulation + Genitals = 69.

"Oh no no no!" Mom's emphatic.

"Ma, you really gotta get out more, you're missing the party," I say with a smile. She gives me the smile back.

Little do we know.

X X X

FRANNIE WAS my professional cherry popper. It's a word-of-mouth business, and between her word and my mouth, I did very well by Frannie. Coma Girl. That's what I call her. She doesn't move a muscle. Doesn't make a sound. I know she's excited because her body does all the things excited women's bodies do: the swelling, the excreting, the hardening and the melting. But she never moves a muscle.

She touches me on the ear with a finger, the signal for me to lie on my back while she crawls up on me, chest to chest, eyes tight shut. She wriggles so she's right at the tip of me. I wrap a hand around the hard bones of her whippet-thin ribs.

Oh God what am I doing? My power fades and I droop limply. I want to go home now. I can't do this.

Change the record, boy!

A Beverly Hills babe's paying you a hundred dollars for sex. You're the loverstudguy. A smile slides across my face, and I'm the star of my own sex movie, as I hear the wackawacka guitar with the basso profundo voice on the soundtrack playing in my head.

"Oh baby . . . give it to me you nasty little baby . . . you love it, don't you, honey? Oh baby, baby, baby."

Suddenly the sixtyminute boy is back on the job.

Frannie grindgrindgrinds until her breath is short; then she hitches shallow gasps, followed by a couple of quick convulsions.

Then she disappears under the covers.

I'm supposed to close my eyes and count to ten. I close my eyes. One Mississippi, two Mississippi, three Mississippi . . . and when I get to ten I open my eyes. Frannie's gone. Dread and anxiety have replaced her. Soiled, unclean, and filthy, I'm overwhelmed by the need to flee. Without even washing Frannie off me, I whip on my clothes, grab the twenty-dollar tip she left beneath the Wedgwood egg, and bolt out the door, head down, guts upside down.

I kick my bike started, and gun it too hard, trying to get the roar to drown out the roar in my head that says how nasty I am. As I slam into gear and skid away, my rape aches. BITCH! FAGGOT! PUNK! I shove it all down, and store it in my meatlocker so it can feed on me later as the hole in my bucket gets a little bigger.

4

SUPERFLY

&

PUPPYLOVE

You can lead a whore to culture but you can't make her think. — Oscar Wilde

A FORTY foot Marlboro Man is roping a cow while sucking on a cigarette looming over the building where the Hollywood Employment Agency sits, smack dab in the middle of Sunset Boulevard. Sunny told me to show up in my GRUNT T with my nuthugging elephantbells at three o'clock on yet another perfect California Tuesday. I didn't know it at the time, but Frannie was a test for me, and this is my reward: an invitation to the Show.

I walk through the door marked HOLLYWOOD EMPLOYMENT AGENCY. The office is generic as a can of beans with "Beans" printed on it. There's no art on the walls of clowns or sailboats or a kitty hanging from a limb by his paws with "Hang in there!" written under it; no "Sound of Music" in muzak; no watercooler to shmooze around; only one nearly invisible couch with one magazine on it and one desk with one phone and one secretary, who has a face you forget even as you're looking at it.

I'm told to sit. No one else is in the waiting area. I pick up the magazine. It's one of those women's magazines with helpful tips on how to store leftovers and quizzes to see if you're compatible with your painintheassbastard husband. I try to read it, but I can't seem to penetrate its glossy surface.

What are you doing? Get the hell out. Now. No, man, you're the loverstudguy, you're here to get the Real Money. More pussy than you can shake a stick at. No. Go call your mother and tell her you want to come home. Yeah, right. She told you to get lost, point blank. They want to give you money for being hot. Shut the hell up and be an American.

X X X

I'M FOUR. "What do you want me to be when I grow up?" I ask my mom. The question takes her by surprise. She stops being a housewife and thinks about it.

"I don't know," she answers.

By the time she was twenty-seven my mom had four children under the age of eight to wrangle into a smooth running unit, but every day she makes a point to spend time with each of us. They hadn't invented the phrase "quality time," but my mother was already spending it with me and my brothers and sisters.

"What do you want me to be when I grow up?" I ask again, in the great tradition of four-year-olds who've asked the same question over and over and over for thousands of years.

"I think," says my mom, "you should do whatever makes you happy."

X X X

MR. HARTLEY is a soft boiled egg with a tan in a gray suit, desk neat as an anal-retentive pin. He looks like he really could be an employment counselor. He certainly doesn't look like a chicken pimp.

"Tell me about yourself," says Mr. Hartley.

"Well . . ."

Rule number four: Say as little as possible. Rule number five: When in doubt say even less. Sunny's voice rings in the belljar of my head. "Just look like ya gotta big dick, boy." I try to construct a well-endowed look on my face, but I'm afraid I look more constipated than hung.

". . . I go to Immaculate Heart College, and I'm a . . . soccer player."

That's as close to large-penised as I can get.

Mr. Hartley nods his head and studies me like I'm a Negro buck for sale at a slave auction. I'm surprised he doesn't put his hands in my mouth and examine my teeth. But I don't resent being evaluated like a slab of beef; I take it as a challenge to prove I'm prime cut.

"I just want to assure you . . . that I'm extremely enthusiastic about working." I lean in and smile, as I imagine having sex with Mr. Hartley's wife, and doing it better than him. "And I will do an excellent job."

Mr. Hartley's caught offguard for a second, and I can see he's the kind of guy who probably isn't very good at sex. Odd that he'd find this job for himself. But the power in the room has shifted, and I have it.

"Are there . . . any things you're . . . uncomfortable with? For example, will you . . . work with men?"

BITCH! FAGGOT! PUNK!

"Actually," I say, "I'm not really interested in working with men."

"Are you sure? Because I can get you a lot of work with men, and you wouldn't have to do anything except let them pleasure you."

Doesn't sound like pleasure to me. Makes me want to fly the chickencoop.

"If you aren't comfortable with that, no problem. Our policy is very strict; we don't ask anyone to do anything they're not comfortable with. We've found our clients and our customers are served better this way. So tell me what you're comfortable with."

What sexual acts am I willing to perform for money that keep me in my comfort zone? The voice that's never wrong is screaming at me to walk and never look back. But I can't move. My brain and my legs are playing tug-of-war and my brain is winning.

"I guess the only thing I'm not comfortable with is men," somehow comes out of me.

Once I accept the fact that I'm willing to have sex for money, basically everything becomes possible, except that which is not a possibility. And the only thing that seems impossible is having some man sexing me.

"Okay, here's how it works," Mr. Hartley's all smoothed out, his engine purring. "We give you a pager. We ask that you keep the pager on you at all times, because this is a first-come first-served business." Only surgeons have pagers. He rattles off a series of little laughs. "When we page you, we ask that you call us back immediately. When you call in, we give you a time, an address, a contact, a dollar amount, and any unusual details you need to know. Once you accept a job, you must perform the job. We're very strict on this point. If you accept a job and do not perform the job, you will not be called again. No drugs, no alcohol. You'll be paid in cash; the customer pays us separately. If you make arrangements with the customer for another date, you must inform us. Failure to do so will result in being immediately dropped from our client list. Is all this clear? Do you have any questions?"

I think for a minute.

"I have one question," I say. "When do I start?"

X X X

"WHY I love America." That's the subject of the essay contest I enter when I'm seven in Hueytown, Alabama.

Here's what I write:

"I love America because she is the greatest country on Earth. In America you can do anything you want if you respect the law. President Johnson is a great president. Governor Wallace is a great governor and

I respect him very much. I love America because everyone is free to respect each other, and any man can be the president. I respect my teachers and my parents. And I respect Alabama. And I love her, too."

✗ ✗ ✗

DAMN MAN, there is a fellow who has definitely mastered the big-dicked look. That's a look I need to cultivate, all full of I-don't-give-a-damn and look-how-big-I-am. As Secretary gives me a pager, I study the guy waiting in the waiting area of the Hollywood Employment Agency. Tight black hair, tight black skin, tight black T, tight black pants, tight black eyes. When I catch his eye I smile. He does not smile back. I make a mental note not to smile so much, because when you don't smile it makes you look like your penis is bigger.

At first the guy seems old. Hard to say how old really. Thirty. Forty. Fifty. They're all the same age to me. The only other age is Really Old, and that's anyone who's about to keel over dead. But as I study him out the corner of my eye, I realize he's not old. He's actually about my age. His oldness is coming from the inside.

"Mr. Hartley will see you now," the secretary says to him. She does not smile. He does not smile. I must stop smiling.

I watch myself studying this manchild who must certainly be a black boy prostitute. When he stands up I'm aware for the first time that this old young fellow is at least a head taller than me. It may be my imagination, but I swear I can see his knob outlined through the too-tight pants, and I'm simultaneously filled with shock and envy.

As I watch him smooth past me with that beautiful Superfly strut, I realize I need to be like him. So easy and so hard, so hungry and so full, so hot and so cool.

I see now that my former strut was wholly inadequate. So as I walk out of the Hollywood Employment Agency I strut a whole new

pumped-up-teenboy-with-a-rocket-in-my-pocket-and-a-lump-of-coal-
in-my-chicken-heart strut.

X X X

EXCITEMENT GRIPS our house. I'm three. Guests are coming over tonight.
My little brother and I are dressed up in our white starchy collary shirts,
blue suspenders, clip-on ties, short knee pants, wee white kneesocks. Our
hairs are combed, our faces washed, and our shoes nice and neat. My
mom's hair is bigger than usual, psoriasis torching on her elbows like
roadside flares at an accident. My dad's joking a mile a minute, roaring
from his crew cut like the factory in his head's working overtime.

I've memorized "The Music Man." I don't know why, I just have. And
now it's my job to get up and sing it for the guests. My mom puts me up
on the vast runway of the living room table, and I'm way up high, in my
English schoolboy finest, those big Guest faces flooding me with warm
wet heat as I sing and dance.

"You got trouble my friends, right here in River City. Trouble with a
capital T and that rhymes with P and that stands for pool—"

Word for word, note for note, just like on the record, all three-year-old
Yankee Doodle Dandy. And when the enormous Guests cheer, laugh,
and clap, and my mom and dad shine at me in the hot spotlight, I am full
and alive and perfectly America.

X X X

IMMACULATE HEART college. Existentialism class. I'm trying to listen to
Sister Tiffany explain how we're free to be whatever we want to be. She's
schooling us on the Myth of Sisyphus. Apparently Sisyphus did some
heinous shit to the gods, so he got sentenced to pushing a big huge rock
up a big huge mountain, every day for the rest of his life. Only when

Sisyphus embraces the rock, becomes the rock, does this futile, pointless, punishing task become his joy.

As a seventeen-year-old boy for rent, I think this shit is deep. I'm bound and determined to find the joy inside my misery. But today I'm having real trouble focusing. All I can feel is that pager in my pocket, big as a garage door opener, resting on my thigh like an invitation to hell. I want it to buzz. I hope it never buzzes.

Sister Tiffany brings me back. Incredible mind this nunbabe has: deep honest funny. No wonder the Catholic Church gave her the heave-ho.

Am I free to make my life whatever I want it to be? I feel trapped between my cock and a hard place, waiting for a date that I desperately need and feverishly fear.

So I stare at Kristy. Helps to stare at Kristy. She's soooooooo cute: small, with a little nose slotted between two big blue eyes blazing under waving brown hair. She's wearing a very loose pheasant-colored peasant shirt, and when I look at her I think Hey, maybe I am free after all. I tail her out of Existentialism class. She smiled at me once during class in a way I was sure meant she wanted to have sex with me. Then again, I'm beginning to think everyone wants to have sex with me.

After class Kristy basks on the immaculate green lawn, and throws her head back in the Hollywood sun like she's in an impressionist painting. Maybe I can make her fall in love with me. Maybe I can move in with her. She can introduce me to her folks. I can help her have a woman's orgasm.

I stop. Breathe. If I can do this, maybe I can plug up some of the holes, stop the bleeding, right the ship. As much as I needed that bucket of chicken in the dumpster, that's how hungry I am for Kristy.

Next thing I know I'm standing over her, trying to look like a loverstudguy and not some scared-to-death dink. Suddenly she realizes someone's standing over her staring, and when she opens her eyes she recognizes me.

A huge long instant follows in which it's unclear whether Kristy wants me to stay, or wants me to piss off. And she seems to be enjoying it, although not in a mean way.

"Hi . . ."

Kristy finally smiles.

"Hi . . ."

I smile.

"How's it goin'?" she asks.

"I'm feeling incredibly existential." This is the first interaction I've had with a woman in a while that didn't involve a nun or a money-for-sex exchange.

"Yeah, those nuns'll kick yer ass," she grins.

"Well, if I have to get my ass kicked, I want it kicked by a nun," I say as I sit. This feels natural. I'm not thinking about my ass. Or my pager. Or my mom.

"I'm just waiting for one of 'em to actually fly into class. I'd convert right then and there, I swear to God." Kristy's definitely putting some flirty spin on the ball.

"I don't think they can actually fly without the whole wimple thing," I spin right back.

"Yeah, I think it's an aerodynamic hand of God situation." Kristy's so normal. So not a freak like me.

I now move directly into the minefield in my mind. What do I do? Ask her if she wants a date? Tell her I'll give her a student discount? Suddenly this fun, sun-filled meeting of a boy and a girl becomes a war zone, and I'm staring into the barrel of my own gun. I'm stuck, struck dumb. I feel the pager cold and hard, and hear its call of the wild. I want to move into Kristy's life and bury myself there. I try to smile. It doesn't work. Then I remember I'm trying not to smile.

"I gotta . . . you know . . . go . . ."

Even as it comes out of my mouth, I know it sounds weird and evasive and not at all the sort of thing that makes a girl fall in love with a boy. I want to buy her a hot chocolate, get her a puppy, tell her who I am. I want to do anything except what I'm about to do, which is run away from this nice normal smart funny loving American girl. I finger my pager, turn my back, and walk away from Kristy.

5

INDUSTRIAL NEW JERSEY

&

GEORGIA

The only abnormality is the incapacity to love. — Anaïs Nin

X X X

"THE MAYOR can go straight to hell. I mean, who does he think he is? You don't just cancel on a dinner party that's been planned for six weeks! The whole reason for the God damn party in the first place was so the mayor could meet all those boring assholes. And my husband, that painintheass-bastard, you know what he said to me? He said, 'Handle it.' I'll give him something to handle, the miserable prick."

Georgia paces and smokes like a nervous chimney. Mr. Hartley told me to be here at four o'clock. It's a hundred-dollar job. Plus a tip, of course. If I get the job done.

TV's on low, so you can barely hear excited people winning money. A painting of a schooner that looks like it's from a starving artist sale sails on the wall. An envelope on a dresser whispers my name.

Georgia lights a new cigarette off the cherry of the one she holds, while another smolders from the ashtray. I smell booze and see the tip of a bottle peeking its head out from a big handbag, like it doesn't want to miss a trick. Next to it a bit of stocking drips. A pair of neon lime shoe twins sit side by side by the side of the bed. Georgia has ten pink piggies painted peach at the end of her fat little feet.

So, she came in, took off her stockings, shoved them into the bag, then knocked back a few snorts to lube the engine, which is always smoking.

Georgia looks like she fell into a trash compactor when she was five foot eleven and didn't escape until she was five foot two. She's wearing a silky shiny neon green knee-length skirt with a silky shiny brown blouse that's at least two sizes too big. The overall effect of Georgia is fleshy, shiny, and smoky.

I'm on the edge of the Cliffs of Hyperventilation, my mind mile-a-minuting, pulse pounding, trying to focus on my breathing. I don't know it at the time, but this turns out to be a very smart move, and when I do manage to track down my breath and force it to get regular, I immediately feel power and control. And Lord, I need power and control right now.

Frannie the Coma Girl. She loves me. Sunny told me so. I see myself in her mirror in my mind, long, muscled and woody. I'm the sixtyminute chicken, star of my own loverstudguy movie.

Georgia motions to the envelope on the anonymous dresser. A hundred-dollar bill lives in there. Making contact with the money is a great balmy calm, and activates the voice in my head:

"Oh baby . . . you love it, don't you? Oh baby, baby, baby."

An adrenaline subway rushes up me, tingly little charges that fire inside, like an addict when the score is knocking on the door. I pose by the mirror. I pose in the chair. I pose by the dresser.

When I catch her eyeballing me, this big bossy brassy ballbusting babe blushes. In real life, I'm so small. Here, I'm so huge, and it's intoxicating.

"Would you mind . . . uh . . . taking off your . . . uh . . . clothes . . ."

Georgia wants me to tell her how pretty she is. Apparently her pain-intheassbastard husband never does.

"You know," I say while I get as naked as I've ever been, "as soon as I walked in, I said to myself, 'She is really pretty.' And you really are. If you were at a party and I saw you I'd definitely hit on you." I come from a long line of toads, and it flows out of me easy as fur pie.

She eats it up with a silver spoon. Asks me to play with myself. Play. Strikes me strange in that moment. Play. Jungle gym and teetertotter. Barbie and G.I. Joe.

So I lie on the bed. And I play. I like watching myself playing in the mirror. And I like the fact that she can't take her eyes off me, but can't look right at me either. The air's filled with sex, and I'm the bullgoose-looney chicken.

I conclude, based upon my very limited database, that women in Hollywood like to watch naked young men masturbate.

My blood is coming to a rolling boil as I play, and if I squint hard enough I can imagine this crazy baby's the beautiful minx star of my loverstudguy movie.

Georgia shuffles over awkwardly, hikes up her skirt and kneels on the bed next to my head, a bouquet of stale cigarette and nasty booze arriving with her.

Suddenly she has one knee on either side of my head. I disappear under the bigtop tent of her neon green skirt, and I'm swallowed up in her dark suffocating circus, where the clowns are scary and the lions unchained.

As her nether underworld zooms in slow motion towards my face, the heat of Georgia blasts me like a furnace, fresh feminine chemicals burning the hairs in my nostrils. It's like a scientist who never actually smelled a woman created an aroma of what female genitals would smell like in a germ-free world. But underneath lurks something dank humid and sordid, like her vagina's been hanging out in a seedy bar too long. I can't breathe. I'm drowning in all this alcohol-saturated smoke-drenched genitalia.

It's all I can do not to throw her off and fly away. But I can't. The son of an Immigrant is here to get the job done. And if I can walk out of this room with a hundred dollars, then at least I'm worth that.

Georgia's planted herself unmoving on my face. A joke pops into my head. As long as I've got a face you've got a place to sit. I make a mental note to laugh about this later.

✗ ✗ ✗

I NEVER went through that "I hate girls" phase so many men never outgrow. I've always been attracted to girls by a force I couldn't quite control.

My girlfriend's name is Sally. I'm five. She has pretty yellow curly hair and blue blue eyes. She wears little flower dresses, a different one every day.

I'm sure she didn't know she was my girlfriend. I showed my love by flying on my bicycle in front of her house over and over, back and forth like some crazed mechanical duck, because I thought I looked so grown up and tough with the wind in my hair, whipping so damn fast past her house.

I sometimes feel like I've spent my whole life riding my bicycle very fast in front of girls' houses, trying to get them to love me.

✗ ✗ ✗

ASPHYXIATION BY vagina. That's what it's going to say on my death certificate, I think, as I suffocate under Georgia. My erection left the party long ago. She hasn't really had a sexual response of any kind, and she's just been using my face as a chair for what seems like months.
I find myself questioning my career choice.

Finally I pull her skirt away from my face so I can breathe. When I do I see Georgia's face as if for the first time, those long sad eyes staring waaaaaaaay off. Damn, what happened to her? She looks down at me. With a mouthful of vagina I ask her if she would like me to stop.

"Would you mind terribly?" she says in a soft little-girl voice I haven't heard coming out of her yet. Then I can see, as if for the first time, how once upon a time Georgia was beautiful. I tell her I really do think she's pretty. She smiles, sighs, climbs down off me, climbs down off the bed, and lights another cigarette.

"Actually, uh . . . I've never had an . . . orgasm."

Georgia's voice has the saddest quiver. She smokes as she doesn't look at me.

I'm not quite sure what to do with this information. I've never been with someone who's paying me to discuss her orgasm issues. But I am enjoying this part of the work much better than being smothered by her toxic pillow of love.

Nakedly, I stand in front of her. I put my hand on her hard stiff hair and hold it there. Reminds me of my mom's hair before she got liberated. Georgia sighs and smiles. There's something familiar about this. Makes me want to bake cookies with Georgia.

I pull her into me and hold her there, feeling her cheek hot against me, smelling her smoky boozy perfume. She takes a deep pull on her fag, and I feel the heat of her cherry on my belly. Hope she doesn't burn me with that thing, I think, as Georgia exhales, smoke escaping like prisoners of war from a concentration camp.

"Do you want to have one?" I ask.

"Yes, I do," Georgia says.

"I can help you with that," I say.

Georgia stops smoking for a moment. She's rag limp and drained dry with wet tears pooling in her eyes. I'm still naked.

"Could you really?" Georgia asks, hope and desperation dancing the cancan in her eyes.

"Sure," I say, "be my pleasure." Even as I flow with compassion and good will, I watch myself calculate how much I can make off this Georgia, the American Dream unfolding right in front of me. I'm making money off other people's misery.

"Maybe we could try this again next week," she says.

"Absolutely," I smile.

She smiles back, her face smooth, loose, and soothed for the first time since I've known her, which is all of about forty-five minutes.

Then something snaps—I can hear it, like a tibia cracking—and a dark thundercloud surrounds Georgia from the inside out. She grabs a cigarette quick, fires her up, and the protective layer of smog covers Georgia again like a cone of silence.

"Jesus, this day is just insane, and if my painintheassbastard husband thinks I'm gonna save his piece-of-shit dinner party, he can kiss my ass."

And on and on.

Georgia slips her neon green shoe twins on her fat little feet, and grabs her big fat bag. She fishes in it for quite a while before reeling out some paper money that writhes around on the hook of her hand. She forks it over mid-monologue. Without looking at it, I say thank you, but I don't think she hears me.

Georgia shakes my hand and leaves.

You sit on a boy's face, then you shake his hand? The more I think about it, the more I realize: That's it in a nutshell, isn't it?

I look at the bill. It's a hundred. A hundred! I open my envelope and extract my other hundred. Two hundred-dollar bills.

I stand there in this Hollywood hotel room, my mouth hanging open like a cartoon dog that's just seen Jesus turn water into a big juicy bone. Two hundred bucks for forty-five minutes of naked sex therapy, some faux cunnilingus, and a small cup of human kindness?

That's Real Money, friends.

X X X

A LITTLE English schoolboy is what I am, please and thank you never far from my pretty little pink lips. I have an English accent until I go to first grade, at which point I drop it so fast I make my own head spin.

When my brother and sisters and I are in the backseat of our faux-woodpaneled station wagon, creating mayhem and wreaking anarchy after the ineffectual sweep of a hand from the front seat misses everyone; after "If you don't quit that bliddy racquet, I'll stop this bliddy car, and you'll bliddy well walk home" has been exposed as the bluff it is; the trump card is always laid down:

"If you don't quit this instant, no Dairy Queen!"

We calm and salivate.

I scream, you scream, we all scream for ice cream.

X X X

ME AND my sex money are all alone. I sink. I have a flash of my mom, and I sink further. I fondle my two hundred, and that makes it better, like a bandage on a kid's booboo. It's not nearly as bad as when Frannie was done with me. I'm already learning to store it away easier.

When I get back home, I can't figure out why I'm so horny and hungry. I call Kristy, but she's not home, and I sink further.

I can't stand still, so I get on my bike, and when I rev loud she leans and growls. Suddenly I'm wandering the aisles of Hollywood Ralph's. I pick out a big dayold birthday cake with pink and blue roses growing in a snowy white pond of sweet lard. I find myself grabbing an industrial-size tub of ice cream.

A spectacularly droopy fiftyish woman in an aggressive orange wig, a skintight leopardprint onepiece bodysuit covered in feline fur, accessorized by big rhinestone-festooned cat glasses—and a scab on her lip—checks me out at the checkout line. She licks her whiskers and hisses, "Go fetch me a pint of milk, I gotta bad hip. I was in *Valley of the Dolls*."

I fetch her milk. The Doll scrutinizes it brutally, then screams right in my face, "Seventy-five cents? For God-damn milk? Ha!!! I can get this for a quarter. I don't want this shit. What the hell is wrong with you?"

She slams the milk into my solar plexus. Then the Doll storms out and disappears back into the Valley, while the hole in my bucket gets a little bigger. I buy the milk. What's cake and ice cream without a little milk to wash it down?

HAPPY BIRTHDAY

Is written in red across the face of my dayold cake, more like a warning than a greeting. It's not my birthday. I'm not happy. A pair of baleful pale plastic anorexic ballerinas on pointe stare at me from atop the field of snowy frosting. I feel an instant, intense attraction to those two beautiful stiff long-legged dancers pirouetting yet forever motionless on this iceberg of a cake. They have the look of Georgia sitting on my face.

When I get home to my hovel, I steamshovel a mouthful of dayold cake into my face; then I cram in a bucketful of ice cream; then I guzzle a gulp of milk. Cake, ice cream, milk; cake, ice cream, milk; cake, ice cream, milk. I'm my own little assembly line, processing milky sugary goo.

The ballerinas stare up at me dolefully and plead with big sadsack plastic eyes: "Please sir, can I have some more?"

Halfway through the cake my taste buds go on a sitdown strike, but I can't stop eating.

And then suddenly there's no cake left. Even the ballerinas are gone. I don't think I ate them, but who knows?

Then I double up with a cramp of wooly mammoth proportions, as my body screams:

"What in God's name is wrong with you?"

Then I plunge like a deep-sea diver into the Sugar Coma Ocean. I see the ballerinas, with their long plastic legs, and sad stiff faces. They're desperate, pregnant, and virgins. They want to stay in my manger. I tell them I don't have a manger. I want to help. I just don't know how.

I lie awake with a thick layer of goop covering my mouth and throat like a mucous overcoat, a nasty black cumulonimbus cloud filling my head, and thunder clapping through the veins in my brain as a lactic sucrose hangover pulses through me.

6

HUEYTOWN

&

THE BLACK SEETHROUGH

FRENCH MAID'S APRON

I loved not yet, yet I loved to love, in love with loving. — St. Augustine

KRISTY WEARS quite tight blue jeans, and a mechanics shirt with the name RUSTY over her Immaculate-Hearted breast. There's something so unrotten about her. So unSunny. Kristy's what I should be doing with my life, that's clear.

Stop. Go over and talk to her, my brain screams, which jumpstarts my legs, which take me to Kristy.

"Hah, Rusty! 'at radiator hose come in yet?" I smile like a cracker drawling at a crawdad hole.

She smiles. So far so good.

"Yeah, but it's gonna cost ya . . ." Is Kristy flirting with me? I think she is. Then again maybe not. It's all so confusing. That's one of the things I like about the chicken work. It's straightforward. You give me this, I give you that. Bada bing bada boom.

"So, uh, the uh . . . well, yeah, I was, see, we're having a, uh, the thing is, a party, yeah we're having a, you know, like . . . party and I, I, I wanted to . . . uh . . ."

If she was paying me for it I could talk all day and all night, but when I'm doing it for me it's like eating taffy with no teeth.

"Okayyyy . . . party? When? Where? Is this an actual invitation?" Kristy's funny.

"Yeah, absolutely. Invitation, right, yes, Friday night, my house. Well, my roommate's apartment actually, but I live there, so, yeah . . ." I can barely get it out.

"Sure," she smiles. Then she walks away.

This girl just buckles my bones.

And she's coming to my party Friday night.

X X X

I'M THE oldest. I was always the oldest. That's how it is when you're the oldest.

I spend my first years in New Jersey. My mother's two sisters have four kids each, just like us, and they live on a dirt road with a lake for a back yard where we spend weekends feasting at a long picnic table on corn on the cob and bangers, burgers and spotted dick, baked beans and Bless This Mess. We swim, we play ball, we have a real good time.

My mother and her two sisters are an inseparable threeheaded bundle of childrearing English immigrant Geordie lassie, finishing each other's sentences, sharing sibling secrets, and laughing in one girly soprano.

Even their pedophile father parked darkly in the corner can't spoil it.

Not for want of trying.

X X X

"CONGRATULATIONS ARE in order, David. Your client was very pleased. She'd like to see you again next week. And we have another job for you,

Friday night, eleven, in the Hollywood hills . . . and this's a two-hour job!"
Mr. Hartley's papa proud. I am a loverstudguy after all.

Then it hits me. Friday. Shit. Party.

"Friday?" I don't sound all excited like I should.

"Is there a problem?" Mr. Hartley asks surprised.

"No. Friday . . . That's . . . great. Sorry, I had, uhm, a thing, but I can
change it. This is great. Thanks . . ."

"Okay, well, good. And I may have something for you Sunday, I'm just
waiting for a confirmation. Any problems?" Mr. Hartley's making sure
my wig is not flipping. I like Mr. Hartley. Well, maybe like is the wrong
word. Admire. The man's a true professional. I'll never see him again, but
I'll always remember that voice.

"No, no, everything's . . . great." I hear it coming out of me, but I don't
feel myself saying it.

Mr. Hartley gives me the four-one-one. Then he's gone.

Shit. Friday night. Kristy, party, two hour job.

I can hear the gods laughing their asses off at me.

X X X

I LOVE the Yankees as only a four-year-old can: the Mick, all power speed
and ease; Roger Maris, the tortured dark prince; Yogi, the swami, number
8, the symbol of infinity sitting on its head; the quirky lefty Whitey Ford,
with the most American name in the world—Whitey—Ford; the mel-
ancholy, hard-working black catcher Elston Howard; the goofy support
group led by Moose Skowron.

Oh what an exciting day it is.

Today my mom and dad are taking me to Yankee Stadium.

X X X

REAL PENNIES in her loafers and sporting little white socks, Kristy floats in rocking a flower dress. Seeing her walk in my door on this Friday party night I want to whisk her into my shithole bedroom and kiss her all over and tell her I'll quit all my crazy shit if she'll let me be hers.

This level of fantasy grips me constantly. It's like my board of directors has walked out en masse, and everyone's running around like chickens with their heads cut off.

I can't walk over to Kristy too fast, or she'll know I'm like, you know, madly in love with her. On the other hand, it's ten o'clock, and I have to leave in forty minutes to go be an industrial sex technician in the Hollywood Hills.

"Hey, can I get you a beer, or a drink, or . . . you know, whatever?" I try not to smile, but I can't help myself.

"Uh, sure, I'll have a cup of whatever." Kristy seems to have no trouble smiling.

"I like your dress. I have one just like it in my closet." That one just eases out nicely. I have to leave in forty minutes. Everything tightens up. God I want to kiss her.

I take her through the small hall that's crammed Hollywood Freeway-at-rush-hour tight, and into the tiny kitchen swarming with Friday night college party bees. I pour her a cup of punch. As the Beatles sing about Mother Mary, and words of wisdom, and times of trouble, I lead Kristy into my roommate's bedroom. It's less crowded in there, and I sure as hell don't want her to see my hell-hole of a room.

She sips her punch.

"How's the whatever?" I ask.

"Excellent. You're not drinking?" she asks.

Seems like the perfect opportunity to feed her my lame excuse about working tonight. But that might just put the kibosh on the whole thing. Maybe I should have my thirty-eight minutes of fun and slip off into the Lone Ranger night. Thinking too much. Just say something, for God's sake.

"No, uh, listen, I'm sorry but I gotta . . . thing that just kinda . . . came up."

"A thing?" She looks at me askance. "What does that mean exactly? A thing? Well, don't you just get more interesting all the time. What are you, a CIA operative? A heroin dealer? A hitman?"

"Actually it's FBI, coke, and money laundering."

"Nice." Kristy looks at me like now she really does want to know what my thing is. And I really want to spill my beans all over her. But I just can't. My beans are locked tight in the cupboard, and I've misplaced the key.

"Seriously, what happened?" she asks.

I can tell if I don't give her some reasonable answer, I can forget Kristy.

"No, what happened was, this guy called in sick, and I have to cover for him."

Kristy thinks for a second, then nods. We talk easy, about nothing really, just thisandthat. At twenty 'til eleven I tell her I've gotta go. I don't do it well. I want to kiss her. I think she wants me to kiss her, but I'm not sure. I'm never sure with her. I keep waiting for her to say, "Oh, just come over when you're done, I'll leave the light on."

But of course she doesn't. In the end I tell her I'll call her, and she smiles in that incredible way girls who've just become women have of smiling. I leave with a limp in my hump and a hitch in my giddy-up to face the piper.

X X X

YANKEE STADIUM makes me quiver with a religious ecstasy of the kind I imagine a young man who grows up to be a priest feels when he first walks in the Vatican. That awe at the vastness of God and the grandeur of man. That feeling of having found something profound and beautiful to believe in.

When I rise with my mom and dad, and forty thousand other Americans, to sing the National Anthem, my dad looks down at me and smiles.

I sit behind one of the pillars in Yankee Stadium, hoping against hope that Yogi will hit a foul ball I can snag. I love peeking out from behind the pillar at all that excitement, an invisible peeping boy.

Mickey Mantle slams a home run in the ninth to win the game, and does the coolest limptrot around the bases, while America goes crazy. And I go crazy with it, right next to my mom and dad.

I limp for about a month after that, trying in vain to perfect that wounded hero Mick thing.

✗ ✗ ✗

THE HOLLYWOOD sign looks close enough to touch from the deck of the house standing on stork legs anchored into the earthquake-friendly hill. The air weighs more than normal as a storm gathers its forces off over the ocean, and heads my way. It never rains in Southern California.

10:59. Friday night. Rule #1: Don't be late. I'm trying to find my breath as I wait for it to be eleven. Trying not to think about kissing Kristy. Trying to see that hundred-dollar tip Georgia gave me.

Ring the doorbell. Stick your finger out and ring the doorbell. Stick it out and ring it.

Somehow the doorbell rings.

A white-skinned freckle-filled red-headed woman in a pink kimono looks me over like I'm a side of pork she can't wait to carve up. I smile. She does not smile. Stop smiling! She lets me in.

On a long brown couch sits a jetblack-haired woman in a blue kimono holding a rose champagne glass. A gigantic plate-glass window stares like an unblinking Cyclops eye at the city of angels, twinkling its billion stars. Janis Joplin's singing my song. She's already dead.

O Lord, won't you buy me a Mercedes Benz?

"Say hello to the boy, Baby," says the jetblack hair in the blue kimono.

"Yes, Sweety," says the redhead in pink. "Hello, boy."

"Tell him where the money is, Baby, " says Sweety.

"The money's on the table, boy," Baby points.

Two hundred-dollar bills sit butch under a fifty.

"And there's another fifty if you play your cards right."

I pocket the two fifty. Hot hot hot.

"Tell him to put on the outfit, Baby," says Sweety.

"Yes, Sweety," says Baby. "Put on the outfit, boy."

Baby hands me a black seethrough apron.

Okay, sure, I can handle this. I start to put the apron on. It's like a costume the sexy maid might wear in a wacky French farce.

Sweety and Baby whisper and giggle. My head gets redhot, like when my dad shaved it too tight and I got sunpoisoning of the scalp.

"Baby, tell the boy he has to take his clothes off before he puts the apron on," Sweety purrs with moneyed condescension.

"Yes, Sweety," says Baby, who translates.

What is it about seeing boys naked that grown women in Hollywood love so much? I wonder as I strip and put on the sheer black seethrough French maid apron, the shame-burn hurting worse.

"Baby, tell the boy to . . ." Sweety milks the pregnancy of her pause.

My head spins with many loverstudguy scenarios: multiple breasts; mouth-watering mouths; sixes and nines; slipping myself in willy-nilly.

". . .Polish the silver," hisses Sweety.

"Oh boy, time to polish the silver," hisses Baby.

I'm sorry, what? Polish the silver? Seriously? POLISH THE SILVER? No, that can't be right.

The customer is always right. So I stand there with my ass flapping in the breeze and I polish the silver, while out the corner of my eye I spy Sweety and Baby swallowing each other like two snakes.

"Tell the boy not to look at us, Baby," Sweety looks at me like I'm beneath scum.

"Don't look over here, boy!" Baby snaps at me.

"I wasn't—" I start to say.

"Tell the boy not to talk, Baby," says Sweety.

"Yes, Sweety," says Baby, who turns to me, cold on cold. "Don't talk, boy, just polish the silver."

So I don't talk. I don't look. I polish the silver. And the thing is, the silver doesn't even need to be polished. It's so shiny you could eat off it.

✗ ✗ ✗

THE YANKEES are coming on TV, and excitement bounds around the walls. I'm five. The living room couch swallows me whole. The TV looks as big as a drive-in movie screen. The National Anthem starts playing, so when my mom and dad stand up, put their hand over their heart, and sing the national anthem with the crowd on the TV, I get up, put my hand over my heart, and sing.

A couple weeks later, I'm at Billy O'Connell's to watch a game with some friends. The national anthem comes on. When I rise, put my hand over my heart, and start to sing, I'm drowned out by the roars of derisive laughter from Billy and his jackals.

I sit quick, burning, horrified at being exposed as an outsider. I never get invited back to Billy O'Connell's.

✗ ✗ ✗

A RED amoeba of hair spreads out over the blue kimono-clad lap of the jetblack-haired Sweety, who moans soft and low, holding Baby's carrottop in her hands between her legs, whispergasping, guiding it first left, then right, like it's her personal joystick. The room is saturated with that beautiful primal love smell, estrogen bouncing off the walls causing muscle memory cramps, cuz my body thinks sex is coming, and my Pavlov dogs are panting, barking, and humping the air.

I stare out at the storm over Hollywood. LA's one big Friday night party. There's even a party at my house—well, the place where I live—and Kristy's dancing with some Joe College guy, which is what I should be doing, as opposed to vacuuming this salmon carpet that's already cleaner than clean, while wearing a seethrough black maid's apron, trying desperately not to look at Sweety and Baby giving each other women's orgasms.

Earlier, I dusted with a feather duster where there was no dust. I Windexed pristine mirrors. I scrubbed the heart of immaculate kitchen-floor grout on my knees with a toothbrush, like some lame softcore Cinderfella.

It's all I can do not to walk over and try to get a guest shot in the Baby and Sweety love show. But of course I can't. I'm the houseboy, guest of honor at this week's meeting of the Man Haters Club. I scowl as I clean while these women feed on my misery.

You wouldn't know it to look at it, but this is even more suffocating than smothering under Georgia.

I can just see my mom's young lover doing this to her—

Change the record, boy.

Two fifty, more if I can just keep my shit together, for cleaning naked? Are you kidding me? Shut the hell up and vacuum.

See . . . the thing is, Kristy . . . I get paid to dress up in women's clothing and do domestic chores while my clients make mad crazy samesex love.

Focus. The big badass vacuum cleaner is state-of-the-art, and has that jet-engine-right-before-takeoff sound. Makes me wish there was some dirt on the carpet to clean.

"Tell the boy to stop vacuuming, Baby. Tell him to turn around and show us his ass," says Sweety.

"Yes, Sweety," says Baby. "Stop vacuuming, boy. Turn around and show us your ass."

I turn off the vacuum cleaner. I have to consciously stop myself from trashing the big folding Japanese screen, shattering the glass window, and smashing the vagina painting that's laughing at me.

Instead I turn around and I show them my ass.

I'm breathing, I'm not looking, I'm trying with all my might to focus on the two hundred and fifty dollars. Fifty more if I'm a good boy. While their gaspy, slurpy, sex breath sounds. It's like radio porn with smell-o-rama.

"Tell the boy to do the dishes, Baby," says Sweety.

"Go do the dishes, boy," says Baby.

Sweety whispers and Baby giggles while I stand in the corner watching myself walk to the sink, turn on the water, soap up a brand new scrubbysponge, and start to wash the big pile of squeaky-clean dishes.

Then I decide, whatever, I'm going to be the best naked boy cleaner in Hollywood. So I throw myself heart and soul into making these dishes sparkle and shine. And it feels good.

Through the gigantic plate-glass window, an electric bucking bronco of brightwhite lightning rides right at me, thunder booms through the universe, and it hits me. I'm pushing that big huge rock up that big huge mountain, knowing it's just gonna roll back down again. And then tomorrow I'm going to do it all over again.

I am Sisyphus, naked in a black seethrough French maid's apron.

7

HARDWIRED INTO KRISTY

I wanna whole lotta love. — Led Zeppelin

X X X

KRISTY'S KITCHEN is warm and tasty. I'm making dinner. For Kristy. At her house. Baby and Sweety are a stain on the other side of the pillow now. I'm grilling onions, garlic, and Italian sausage for Kristy. I'm convinced this is what it smells like in heaven. We're talking about nothing really, just easy talk, thisandthat. We're drinking some fifteen-dollar-a-bottle red wine I bought with my prostitute money. It seemed like such a huge amount of money, and I felt like such a big boy buying it, the son of immigrants making good in this brave new world of swimming pools and movie stars. And the clerk didn't even ask for an ID, which I took as a very good sign.

The fifteen-dollar wine is making it even warmer in the kitchen. I'm going to make this girl fall in love with me, and it kills me. I could move right in here. And if things got a little rough we could always borrow money from her folks, or even move in with them, God forbid; but if we had to, we could. Barbecue by the pool on Sunday afternoon. Getting some fatherly advice from her old man. "Can I call you, Dad?" "Why sure, sonny . . ."

Kristy's wearing a Bullwinkle T. I do a wicked Bullwinkle, so I trot it out for her, that deep dumb cartoony singsong: "Hey Rocky, watch me pull a rabbit out of my hat. Nothing up my sleeve—" (Sleeve rip) "Presto!" (Roooooooar!) "Oops, wrong sleeve."

Kristy lets loose a gutbusting blast of laugh that makes me believe I just might be free after all.

Candles burn. Scarves are tied around bedposts and headboard. Joan of Arc, Joni Mitchell, Billie Holiday, Eleanor Roosevelt, and Babe Didrickson are stuck on her walls hearing voices from God, fingering a guitar, moaning the blues, being the First Lady, and sinking a twenty-footer.

Ethel Merman sings on the stereo—

There's no business like show business like no business I know!

✗ ✗ ✗

I COME home from school to find my mother stained with tears, which rain down her white-hot face. My little six-year-old heart sinks like a fat rock as she sits me down on that vast reservoir of a couch and sobs, shoulders shaking like an earthquake's cracking her dam.

We're m-m-m-moving, to Alab-b-b-b-bama.

Judging by her reaction it sounds like a very bad place to be moving. I want to make everything better. I take her wet hand. Kiss her humid cheek. I'm being the best six-year-old husband I can. And learning valuable chicken skills.

So my dad hauls us all to the dark heart of the Deep South where he runs a factory for his explosives company. Our All-American rocket-ship crashlands in Hueytown, Alabama, one of three sister cities south of Birmingham: Hueytown, Louietown and Deweytown, the only towns in America named after cartoon ducks.

I want to be an American, and in Hueytown, Alabama, circa 1965, this means being a Bear Bryant-worshipping, cross-burning, sheet-wearing, Confederacy-loving good ol' boy.

X X X

PURPLE FLOWERS in a yellow vase sit on Kristy's polished mahogany dresser. "Truth is beauty and beauty truth, and this is all ye need know" is calligraphed on a piece of paper stuck on her wall. John Keats, who wrote those words, died when he was twenty-two. I figure I still have a good couple of years left to do something great.

I'm sitting on Kristy's bed. We're in the neighborhood of four AM, and it's a very exciting neighborhood. She tells me about Marty her German shepherd, who sleeps with her when she's home. I see myself in her parent's backyard playing fetch with Marty. Kristy tells me about her little sister Rhonda who tried to commit suicide—only she wasn't really trying to kill herself, it was actually just a cry for help. I see myself sitting on young Rhonda's bed, earnestly helping her overcome her depression, to the eternal gratitude of her adoring parents.

I feel like I could sit on Kristy's bed for the rest of my life listening to her talk. And she asks about my stories, so I tell her some of them, and she laughs in all the right places.

Then Kristy tells me she's tired. I don't move a muscle. She's gonna have to call AAA and have my ass towed out of there.

"So, uh . . . you wanna crash here?"

BITCH! FAGGOT! PUNK!

I see SEXY:

"You wanna crash here?"

I see myself slicing off his offending member and stuffing his throat with it. I see myself driving back up the hills very quietly, breaking into Baby and Sweety's house dressed in a Richard Nixon mask, and wreaking my furious vengeance upon them.

Kristy doesn't sound nearly as casual as she thinks she does when she says it again:

"So, uh . . . you wanna crash here?"

I rocket back into my body and try to be all whatever: "Sure." While pinwheels turn cartwheels in my head.

Kristy disappears into the bathroom. I honeymoon swoon on her bed. I shake my head. Let out some air. Maybe I really can leave all this chicken shit behind. I don't have to do it if I don't want to. I'm here now, aren't I?

Crashing with Kristy.

X X X

GEORGE WALLACE Elementary School buzzes busy with little southern bees, while I try not to look like my seven-year-old new-boy hands are two sizes too big, waiting for the morning bell with gobs of gradeschoolers in little Alabaman cliques, surrounded on the wallflower fringes by the fat, the hopeless, and the future millionaires.

"Where'd you get that sweater?" somebody asks Jordan Baylor, my cool cracker classmate.

"Stoled it awffa dead nigger," he drawls.

Everyone laughs.

Without thinking I say, "It's not nice to call black people niggers."

"What are you, a nigger lover? Hey nigger lover!" Jordan Baylor, the cool kid, turns on me, hissing in that Ku Klux Klan Youth way.

"Hey, nigger lover!"

Everyone yells—

"NIGGER LOVER!!! NIGGER LOVER!!!"

Someone spits on me. Everyone laughs again.

I'm ashamed that I repeated what my mom told me, embarrassed and exposed as a One-of-Them. But my upper lip is trained British stiff, and never quivers.

The bell rings, and everyone whips into George Wallace Elementary School. I wipe the spit off. It's cold and slimy.

The next time someone asks me where I got something, I say, "Stoled it awffa dead nigger."

Everyone laughs.

✕ ✕ ✕

"WANNA CRASH on the couch . . . or in here?" Kristy's light as meringue. "I'll crash here, but I'm warning you, no funny business." I get the laugh. One thing about being a chicken, it makes you cool in the fray.

"That's too bad." She half smirks, "I was gonna break out the scuba gear and the chaps."

I don't volunteer that I was recently in a seethrough French maid's apron. Kristy wears a flannelly nightie, soft as babies, and smells of soap and lotion.

My shoes and socks are off, but my nuthugging elephantbells and my skintight Malcolm X T are still on. She's under her yellow lamby comforter and ivory sweet sheets.

I slip under with her, and oh, it's good baking in all that warm essence of Kristy.

"Spoon?" I whisper.

Kristy turns her back and snuggles into me. I put my arm around her middle, fit my nooks into her crannies, and my crannies into her nooks. She puts her hand on my hand on her flat belly, and I dive into the smell of her hair. This is almost better than sex.

Almost.

I try not to move. I breathe. I'm trying to be still so I can soak it all in, but the gravitational pull of her womb is sucking me like the tide towards her moon.

Then, through no effort on my part, I feel myself begin to inflate, until I'm stiff as a wooden Indian. Still I don't move, waiting, enjoying this kid-on-Christmas-morning feeling, separated from Kristy by one thin layer of nuthugging elephantbells and a little flannel nightie.

Kristy wiggles. Not much mind you, but it's a clear wiggle, followed by a wrapping and a squeezing.

Suddenly hands are on skin, T is stripped off, nuthuggers are slid out of, and after many sweet deep kisses, I'm eye to eye with the pungent glory of Kristy.

I breathe her in. I breathe her out.

In. Out. In. Out.

No chemicals here. No cigarettes, no booze, no abuse. Kristy smells like life itself. I'm lovedrunk, the tip of my tongue hardwired into her sweet center.

This is so different from working sex. That's dank dark distant and mechanical, and I have to pump myself up into a loverstudguy to do it.

Here, now, when Kristy finally lets go all over me, I feel at one with the universe. I move up the bed and take her in my arms.

I don't even care if I have intercourse with her.

I want to move in with her.

And now that Kristy knows just how good I am, I'm sure it's only a matter of time before I'm having that barbecue with her parents, and throwing a bone to Marty.

8

GODZILLA

&

KING DONG

You who desired so much—in vain to ask
Yet fed your hunger like an endless task. — George Crabbe

"THAT PAININTHEASSBASTARD husband of mine's driving me crazy. He's trying to hire his little chippy. Executive assistant—ha! Executive cocksucker more like it. If I didn't have a pre-nup, I'd divorce that miserable prick so fast it'd make his balls spin."

Same time. Same channel. Next week. Georgia's still smoking, this time in a loose puce housedressy thing and flat black shoes.

There was no hello from Georgia. She keeps watching me, but she hasn't looked in my eyes yet, like I'm a male Medusa lovemonster you must avert your eyes from lest you turn into a pillar of salt or stone.

As Georgia yammers, I have a flash of waking up in Kristy's bed the morning after our crashing. In the harsh light of day the scarves seemed pretentious, the pictures on the wall schoolgirly in the worst way. In fact, the room seemed like a pampered silverspoon princess room. Bet she never fried no chicken. Bet she never put on the seethrough maid's uniform and had to show someone her naked ass. Suddenly Kristy didn't seem so hot or pretty or cute. Her nose seemed a little pinched, her lips a little thin, her ass too big and tits too small. A hair growing out of her left breast was really starting to annoy me. I wanted to get the hell out of there as bad as if she was a trick, and when Kristy offered to make me breakfast, I almost jumped out of my skintight Malcolm X T. I was trying to be coolcalmcollected about the whole thing, but my heebees were having geebees. I told her I couldn't have breakfast cuz I had a job interview. I had to work that night, but I'd call her when I got off; maybe we could hang out.

There was no job interview. I wasn't working that night. I was going to a party at Sunny's, a 3D Fellini freakshow. And I was definitely not inviting Kristy.

I could feel her moving away, wondering if I'm weird damaged goods she should just cut loose now, before it's too late. Who the hell am I, anyway? Some whore. My guts tugged. Suddenly I'd never wanted anything more in my life.

"Hey, I had a great time last night," I pulled her into me. I kissed her neck, my brain turning off and my body turning on. "You know, I was thinking, maybe you should be breakfast." I snapped right into Mr. Loverstudguy without even knowing it.

I fell into her bed and pulled Kristy down with me. She laughed. Now we were back on it. I kissed her lips, which were suddenly not so thin anymore, and I put my hands on her ass, which was suddenly just right. Kristy was great for breakfast. Then I pretended to make a phone call to re-schedule the job interview I didn't really have, and took her out to breakfast with my sexmoney. It was official. Kristy and I were a couple.

Then what am I doing here now with Georgia?

"I'm sorry, what'd you say?" I say.

"I said, I want to work on . . . that thing we talked about last week." Georgia's shy high little-girl voice sucks me back to this Hollywood hotel room as she lights another cigarette.

I'm skeptical about Georgia ever having an orgasm. Hell, she can't even say the word. But I'm certainly willing to give it the old college try. For a hundred bucks.

"Sure," I slip her a sly smile that says if anyone can help her have one, it's me.

I can feel Georgia's gaze hot on my legs and stomach and ass. There's no sex in her glance, but she does seem very interested in looking at me, like I'm an exotic animal at the zoo.

Did I mention I'm naked again?

"Why don't you lie down on the bed?" I flip off the lights.

She gets on her back on the bed, and I put my head between her legs. This is better. I can breathe this time, which helps no matter what line of work you're in.

I take her hand, place her fingers between her legs and move them gently, trying to prime her pump. But when I remove my hand, her digits sit there like a limp fishstick.

Oh my, this is a dry place to grow a flower of love. Gallons of water, summers of sun, and tons of shit will be required. There's a hundred-dollar bill laughing in my pocket.

It's like kissing dead flesh sprayed with Lemon Pledge. I work and I work and I work, but the jaws of of life can't pry her out of the wreckage, and mouth-to-mouth is not working. Georgia's vagina has arrived DOA.

The great thing about cunnilingus as opposed to intercourse for a boy chicken is that the erection is superfluous, so the mind can wander without repercussion. So as I continue to try to resuscitate Georgia's Sleeping Beauty, I time-travel to Sunny's party. Maybe some crazy young girlygirl'll show me the meaning of life. Kristy's sitting at home. What would she think if she saw me here now on this bed between Georgia's legs? She'd flush me like a soiled toilet.

X X X

DAD LOVED smoking and taking home movies, and he did them both relent-lessly. His 8mm Bell & Howell had a klieg light on top you could use to scan the exercise yard at Sing Sing, so in our home movies we squint stiff, grinning gamely like bad TV-movie-of-the-week actors trying to portray a happy family. And it's silent, so there's no chirruppy little Christmas sounds coming out of the jittery surreal family, captured like bugs in amber.

I'm four, it's Christmas morning, and the industrial-strength light is burning a hole in my little corneas as I swim in an ocean of GI Joes, sport-ing goods, and little stuffed dogs.

I spot my little Roy Rogers cowboy outfit. It gets no cooler than that for a four-year-old boy. I put on my little ten-gallon hat, slip on my little holster, and ease my guns in. Sharp I turn, a gunslinger squinting into the high-noon OK Corral Christmas morning searchlight. I draw, whipping out my six-shooter, and rapidfire the trigger with my left palm while aiming straight into the camera, blasting away rat-a-tat-tat, blazing bullets at the smoking dad behind the camera.

Bam! I'm hit, plugged with hot lead. My gun falls in slow motion, I clutch my wee breast, sway painfully, then drop, and writhe on the floor in heroic American agony.

Then my whole body goes limp. It's peaceful in the womb of death, eyes closed to the roaring smoky spotlight. I lie there for a long time on the floor.

Dead.

X X X

Life is so peculiar—shoo be do wop do wah!

LOUIS ARMSTRONG sings; the gumbo's got a big hot kick, and they ain't nobody here but us chickens. 3D's become my home away from home.

Although what home I'm away from is unclear. Sunny's my mothersuperior-daddydearest bigbrother, but in the back of my mind I suspect I'm only here because I'm making him money.

He asks all about Baby and Sweety. Apparently he knows them socially, and his pink's so tickled by my tale he can't help but shout out, "Hoooo-ie! Ain't that some shit!" and a good old fashioned "Eh toi!"

It's fun telling my war story in this Fraternity of Freaks.

Sunny gives me the skinny on my fellow chickens and chickadees:

Dave's six-foot-two, a long, lean, gorgeous orphan who survived institutionalized sexual molestation and will service anything that moves. Actually, it doesn't have to move: if you pay Dave, he'll shtup it.

Laura's not quite five feet, not quite ninety pounds, half-Cherokee, half-Irish, half-Swedish. I say that's one half too many. Sunny says, "You don't know Laura." She survived a mother who burned her with cigarettes, matches, candles. She hates men, hates women, and loves pain.

Cruella's six-foot-four and so black she's almost blue. She's got huge fake breasts, but everything else is real. Decked out in a sparkly evening gown with a slit that goes all the way up to there, she flashes incredible Betty Grable legs. If Betty Grable were a six-four black transsexual. She was found in a trash can when she was three days old. We talk about switchhitting. Baseball, not sex. Turns out Cruella was an All-Star catcher in Little League. Just like me. We make plans to take in a Dodgers game. One of my great regrets is that I never took in a Dodgers game with the crossdressing Cruella.

Billyboy and Bobbygirl are sweet sixteenish. They're Dixie chickens, identical looking redheads. They survived being very successful commercial actor kids until they were thirteen, when their alcoholic father stole all their money and ran off with a model. Dad's in the process of drinking himself to death, and succeeding very well, apparently. They finish each other's sentences, and are perhaps the most charming people I've ever met. They're great favorites of Sunny, as cash cows tend to be, and he treats them like long-lost inbred family. They're trying to sell a sitcom based on their life, and apparently NBC is interested.

We're one big happy nasty family, and I bask in the creepy comfort of it.

X X X

VACATIONING IN a Wild West ghost town. I'm ten. I've been looking forward to this for weeks, my mind alive with visions of Billy the Kid, Wild Bill Hickock, and Wyatt Earp, with the great Roy Rogers singing on Trigger.

But it's nothing like that. Just old dead buildings. Not wild at all. No ghosts.

My father, my brother, and my two sisters pose American Gothic for a family snapshot on a platform atop a scaffold the hangman used for executing cattle rustlers and lowdown no-account murderous thieves and such.

I'm standing slightly apart from everyone, noose around my neck, eyes bugging and arms stiff, a goofball kid criminal being hanged to death.

I've progressed from being shot at Christmas to hanging in the Old West.

X X X

GODZILLA IS his name. He's the guy I saw in the Hollywood Employment Agency waiting room. I thought I'd see him in 3D, and here he is. Godzilla. He's still tight and black, but it turns out that under all that dark ice he's like an oversized goofy twelve-year-old, telling a story, or laughing at a joke, or saying hey to a friend. Then the next second he's an old man.

Sunny introduces me to Godzilla. "Show the boy why they cawll ya Godzilla," Sunny laughs.

Godzilla smiles like he wants to be begged.

So Sunny begs.

"Git it out! Come on, everybody . . . It's showtime!"

Everyone gathers around Godzilla, who gets a funny crooked smile on his face with a trace of sad behind it. He likes the attention, you can tell, but at the same time, I can see that he feels like a freak among freaks.

"Listen hear G, ya better git that badboy out, or there's gonna be trouble here ta-night!" Sunny's the ringmaster of bawdy debauchery, fueling the abused teenage hormones bouncing around 3D.

Finally Godzilla unzips, fishes dramatically, and folds it out.

A baby's arm with an apple in the fist. I believe that's Tennessee Williams, but I'm not sure. Veins bulging like a relief map of the Amazon, it must weigh thirty pounds, and looks like it'd take all the blood in his body just to fill it up. It's a cock that could launch a thousand ships. The crowd gasps, agape at the magnitude of the thing. I am floored, like when I saw the Grand Canyon for the first time.

Turns out Godzilla's been making money with it since he was ten years old, when his big sister charged her friends a quarter to look at it. By the time he was fourteen, that extraordinary organ was supporting his whole family. No one knows how old he is, but he makes a very good dollar.

Man, woman, doesn't make any difference—if you got coin, you can have some kind of sex with Godzilla. It takes a lot of money for him to actually put it in you, but you can pay to look at it, or touch it, or whatever else you want. If you pay, Godzilla will play.

He launches into a story about some trick who paid him three Gs to rub his thing on the guy's feet. He says it was a good business lesson, because he didn't want to do it, so he kept saying no, and the more he said no, the more money the trick offered him, until suddenly he was at three Gs, and he said yes. Turns out it was the easiest money he ever made: he rubbed it on the trick's feet for about thirty seconds, the freak cums, and that's it. He says he felt so bad taking all that money he almost gave some of it back.

Almost.

He waits a long time for the second "almost," and he gets the big laugh.

"Three grand for thirty seconds' work ... damn, my mama'd be proud. She always said I'd make it in the white man's world."

I'm pretty sure I saw Godzilla years later on the box of a pornographic movie, dressed as an old-time king surrounded by five or six very big-haired big-breasted babes staring struck dumb at his monument to manhood. He was wearing a crown, and that same sad sly crooked smile I saw that night in 3D.

I smiled when I saw that box. There's Godzilla, making it in the white man's world. And the name of the movie, I believe, was *King Dong*.

Turns out Godzilla's real name is Gordon.

X X X

LULU IS our maid in Hueytown. She's a deep black woman with a molasses heart and a warm well of patience, good sense and human kindness. She introduces us to the rapture of barbecue chicken, the smoldering majesty of blackeyed peas, and the soothing beauty of sweet potato pie.

Lulu brings us baked goodies that make you glad you were born, and my mom gives her clothes and books for her kids. The other families make their maids take the bus home, but my mom often drives Lulu in our faux-woodpaneled station wagon.

When we cross the railroad tracks into Coon Town, as my schoolmates at George Wallace Elementary School call it, I see big huge cars parked in front of crippled shanties with FOR RENT signs on them. Looking at those beat-to-shit, ramshackled shacks my ten-year-old brain thinks, "Who in their right mind would want to rent a place like that, and why is there a shiny new car in front of it?"

Row after row of busted-up hovels and barefoot chilluns running with scrawny chickens pecking in dusty front yards next to nasty-looking skinny-ribbed dogs sniffing around for something to eat. When I see footage years later of Shantytown in apartheid-era South Africa, I'm reminded of taking Lulu home to the wrong side of the tracks.

My mom loved Lulu because Lulu was a remarkable woman who was managing to thrive in a hostile environment. It never dawned on my mother to consider what color Lulu was.

✗ ✗ ✗

JADE WEARS a red leather micromini and a tiny red T that stops two inches above her belly button. She wears no shoes. Her hair is long and straight and shines like midnight oil. She's little, but she takes up a lot of room dancing in the corner by herself, doing a hybrid kabuki-geisha-hustle as Jimi Hendrix plays "Foxy Lady." She looks tough, like she doesn't need anything or anyone, but freaky, like you could ask her to blow you on the White House lawn, and if she was in the right mood she'd do it. Turns out this is very close to the truth. She materialized out of the thinnest air. I don't know anything about her, but I've already fallen deeply sweetly madly in love with her.

Kristy can't dance like that.

When Sunny witnesses my Jade swoon, he leans in way close, puts his hand on my chest above my heart, his lips sucking distance from my ear, and whispers like my guardian devil:

"Don't even think 'bouttit, boy!"

"Who is she?" I'm a man hearing what he wants to hear and disregarding the rest.

"No, baby Ah know my lips was movin' but somehow the woids didn't make it to your ears. Ah said, 'Don't. Even. Think. 'bouttit.'"

He gets his Serious Sunny face on. It's the same face he put on when he told me not to pull anything funny with the Hollywood Employment Agency, cuz they were people who would seriously kill you. Get the money up front.

"Goil messed up," Sunny says.

"We're all messed up, Sunny," I say.

"Yeah, but that goil MESSED UP!" Sunny says.

"Okay, you warned me. Now who is she?" I am persistent and stupid holding hands.

"She Jade," says Sunny.

Jade.

With the money she's probably making and the money I'm making, we could get a bitching apartment, a nasty car, a killer Harley, and we could have crazy freaky sex every day. How cool would that be? I can see the whole thing so clearly.

Jade.

9

JADE

Love stinks. — The Ramones

X X X

TOOLING UP the Pacific Coast Highway with the top down in the pink of Jade's convertible, cool seasalty air breezing our hair, the moon shining on the ocean and "Good Vibrations" washing over us from the radio, I've never been happier to be an American.

Jade's not her real name. She never tells me her real name. I never ask. No one knows where she lives. She doesn't say anything, hasn't spoken since we left the party. The only reason I know her name's Jade is because Sunny told me so. In fact the only thing she said to me all night was, "You wanna go for a ride?"

I lit up like a Christmas tree at Rockefeller Center, trailing her out the door faster than you can say, "Heel, boy!"

I caught Sunny giving me his you're-an-idiot-to-walk-out-that-door-with-that-girl look, but all I could do was shrug him a whattayagonnado? smile as I was swept like a felled tree down Jade's flume.

One part of me wants her to talk, wants to know how this girl got to be Jade. But another part of me just doesn't want to hear all her weepy stories, doesn't want to tell her mine.

Then I remember reading in a magazine that living the High Life is just a state of mind. If you think you're living the High Life, ipso facto, presto chango, you're living the High Life. I have large cash money in my pocket. I'm roaring up the Pacific Coast Highway with all this Jade. I'm living the High Life.

But Kristy's sitting in the livingroom of my mind. I should call her. I don't wanna call her. I don't need her.

I have Jade.

X X X

AFTER CHURCH one Sunday when I'm ten, my dad pulls me aside, and there with Jesus Christ Our Lord and Savior nailed to the cross and bleeding for my sins right over my head, he says, "Son, one day you'll fall in love with a nice girl, and, well . . .you'll want to make love to her. You'll know you're in love because your organ will become engorged with blood . . . Your partner's whatsit will secrete a thick lubricant . . .You'll mount her, penetrate, and thrust until you ejaculate your spermatozoa. The good news, son, is that if it's done properly, you can get the whole thing over with in less than a minute!"

I'm sure that's not actually what he said, but that's what I heard.

X X X

ENCASED IN steel and glass, I can see the Pacific Ocean waving at me all the way from Japan. I don't know whose place this is, or why Jade has the key, or even where the hell I am for that matter.

But I am definitely living the High Life.

Jade Asian-handmaiden lapdances all around me. She still hasn't spoken a word since we left, and the more she doesn't say anything, the more normal it seems, and the more I like it. All those words. What's the point?

Jade lays out her equipment with the precision of an alchemist. Lights her candle. Lays her spike on the table. Dumps her white powder into her spoon. Floats her spoon under flame until her white powder melts into a spermy liquid. Draws clear liquid meticulously through the filter of a cigarette into her spike.

Today, kids, Mr. Wizard's gonna teach you how to shoot heroin.

Jade lifts her skirt, finds a nice spot on her bottom, slides the spike into it, and slowly pumps a river of junk into her hungry ass. Then she unplugs the spike, sets the works down on the table, and slowly the sleepy sweetness sweeps through her. Her head lolligags like a nodding bobblehead doll in the back of an old Chevy, her eyes drift off into the sunset, and she strolls off down Big Easy Street.

She looks into me. She wants me to come over.

The lady or the tiger.

In a heroin haze Jade pulls on me, so my beltbuckle ends up next to her mouth. Looking down at her, I'm struck by how exquisitely absent she is. Part of her allure is physical, certainly, but part of it comes from the fact that she is just so far away. I want to reach down inside and pull her out.

Jade makes me her human pacifier, moaning low in the back of her throat like a big cat purring. Later I'll find out she charges a thousand dollars an hour, and for that you can do whatever you want to Jade. She could work twenty-four-seven if she wanted, but she only calls Sunny when she needs it. Sometimes she calls ten times in a day, sometimes once in a month.

Somebody tells me later she's from some millionaire family in the Orient. Somebody else says she's the daughter of a Yakuza hired-killer heroin dealer. Somebody tells me she's an orphan from Shaker Heights, a suburb of Cleveland, Ohio.

Jade brings me just to the edge and takes me back over and over, jacked right into my pleasure centers. Everything shuts out except Jade.

We have all our clothes on the whole time. Strange, I think: at this point in my life I work naked and have sex with my clothes on.

Jade reaches in her little bag she always carries with her, and out pulls something I can't see.

OH GOD!

It's a razorblade! I see me walking into the emergency room with my severed member in my hand. I see Sunny shaking his head going, "Ah wahned ya, boy!"

It's not a razorblade. It's some lubey thing that makes me slip right into Jade, and she squeezes me like I'm dough she's kneading with her vagina.

Jade wants me to bodyslam her. So I am her madman, and I ram her with everything I've got. Her body goes dead limp, and she makes the same animal throat noises she was making before. She's my Junky Raggedy Anne and I'm her Loverstudguy Andy.

Finally, when I let myself go, I shake like I'm attached to an industrial-strength paint mixer, ten point oh on the Richter scale, and leave my mind behind, screaming and wailing.

When I parachute back down, she's kind of whimpering. I'm proud I could rock this girl's world. Then I realize it's not a sex whimper. Jade's crying.

All of a sudden she doesn't seem like some hot mysterious flower of the East. She seems like a sad broken little heroin addict prostitute girl. What am I doing here? What am I doing? I want to go now. I want to be in my own bed. I want to be in my own life.

Jade disengages, collapses, and lapses into a deep sleep before she even hits the pillow, like she was shot by a sniper with a silencer.

Morning after, Jade's gone. I search the whole house, but Jade's gone. I have a little-boy panic, synapses twitching with the memory of searching a vacant house for my mother.

Stop. Breathe. I put together another emergency meeting of the What Am I Gonna Do? Committee and decide to call Sunny, who comes and gets me, bitching and moaning the whole time with a litany of I-told-you-so's and when-will-you-ever-listen-to-me's, essential ingredients in any humble pie.

In the future, when I yearn for her, I remind myself of the long ride back to apartment 3D, with that cold jangled abandoned feeling of being ditched by Jade.

10

BABA RAM

WAMMALAMMA DINGDONG

It is not only our fate but our business to lose innocence, and once we have lost that, it is futile to attempt a picnic in Eden. — Elizabeth Bowen

x x x

LAUREL CANYON is an enchanted eucalyptus oasis in the middle of this Hollywood smogfarm metropolis. As I enter the log cabin house set behind a wildflower jasmine jungle, a solid block of patchouli incense musk nearly knocks me over. With driftwood tie-dye batik beanbags windchimes macramé hanging plants and Mexican Day-of-the-Dead skeleton art everywhere, it looks like Woodstock exploded in Rainbow's house.

Driving that train, high on cocaine, Casey Jones, you better watch your speed . . .

Jams through the room.

Rainbow has long straight grey hair, wears feather earrings and a floor-length tie-dye dress with a dopey hippie happy face on it. No make-up. No shoes.

"Namaste. Enter. Would you like some ginseng tea?" wafts out of Rainbow.

The customer's always right. When in Rome, drink ginseng tea. While she fetches me tea I survey lots of pots of pot plants. And cats. I count four, but I feel the presence of many more, and when I close my eyes I smell cat hanging under that pagan lovechild aroma.

Rainbow returns with my tea in a psychedelic homemade mug with a drawing of some dopey hippie happy face on it. The tea smells too earthy and dank for drinking, but I bring the Mother Earth medicine scent up to my lips and sip.

It's good. And good for me.

"Do you dig the dead?"

Rainbow's looking at me like she expects something. I'm confused. Is this some weird necrophilia deal Mr. Hartley forgot to tell me about? I make a mental note: Find out what's the going rate for having sex with dead people. Do I feel comfortable fucking a dead person? Coma Girl's dead yet sexed-up face flashes.

"I believe Jerry Garcia is the physical embodiment of the Godhead, don't you?"

Jerry Garcia! The Grateful Dead. That's who belongs to that dopey hippie happy face. Jerry Garcia! I see me digging a grave and putting a gratefully dead Jerry Garcia in it.

"Oh yeah, Jerry Garcia is a total Godhead. Yeah, I definitely dig the Dead . . ."

I trot out my best hippieboy smile. Actually, I could care less about the Dead. Or the dead. Rule #5: The customer is always right. I'm here to get paid. I look around for my envelope. No envelope. I don't like that. I'm looking for a low-maintenance score, get in, get out, bada bing bada boom. Relax, cowboy, you're gonna get paid, go with the flow, flowing, in the flow. Hey, someone wants to pay me to say Jerry Garcia is the physical embodiment of the Godhead, that's Easy Money.

"Give me your hand," says Rainbow.

I give her the hand. She takes it.

"You have big hands," she says.

In my line of work that's a compliment.

"Thank you," I say.

She looks at me funny, like it wasn't a compliment at all, just a statement of fact. But she doesn't really seem to care, she's looking into my palm like it holds the key to the sweet mysteries of life.

GET THE MONEY UP FRONT

GET THE MONEY UP FRONT

GET THE MONEY UP FRONT

Only the newest greenhorn in Greenhornville doesn't get the money up front. This is what separates the rank amateur from the hard-working professional. You're not here to have a good time, Charley, you're here to get paid.

But Rainbow has produced nothing, and I can tell she'd be just the sort who'd get all bent if a guy mentioned something as crass as cash.

So I sit and stew as Rainbow gazes into the crystal ball of my palm.

X X X

NEWBIE NEWBOY I am again at thirteen. Since none of these Dallas hayseeds'll give me the time of day, I find myself staring through the window of life at the party where everyone's having a marvelous time.

In English class the teacher announces she wants to do a dramatic reenactment of *The Diary of Anne Frank*, the heart-wrenching tale of one girl's humanity shining in the face of unthinkable evil. Volunteers for acting in Teacher's pet project will get extra credit. Whoever's interested should come when school's over at three to audition.

Anne Frank don't make me no never mind, as they say in Big D. But the whole rest of the day, that voice which is never wrong keeps whispering that I should show up.

At three o'clock, six of the hottiest of hotty thirteen-year-old babies in Lyndon Baines Johnson Junior High School sit in English class arguing about who's best suited to play Anne Frank, our tragic doomed heroine. My mouth drops open. My tongue plops out. It's all I can do not to bust out laughing as I slide like a fox into the debutante henhouse.

X X X

STARING STILL at my palm, Rainbow is now starting to seem demented. I'm convinced she's a Charlie Manson groupie with a garotte she's gonna use to sacrifice me and the goat I'm sure is in the backyard.

I'm starting to have serious doubts about Rainbow. About this whole line of work. I've got enough money. I could excuse myself like I'm going to the bathroom and walk out and just drive. But again the question: Where? My mom in Oregon? Dad in Dallas? Nobody wants me. I don't tell anyone. I can't ask.

"You're a very old soul . . ." concludes Rainbow.

You said a mouthful there, sister.

". . . and you've lived many lives . . . You were an explorer and sailed all over the world . . . and you were a sultan with many women. You were a mighty warrior in battle, and you were a slave on a plantation . . ."

Rainbow looks into me like she has periscopes that go through my eyes.

That's when I notice her for the first time. In all the confusion I haven't really seen her. She has deep eyes, steel-colored with flecks of cobalt. A big Scandihoovian Bergman madly suffering but eternally hopeful face. I half expect Death to walk out of her bedroom and challenge me to a game of chess for my soul.

"You're here to learn a lesson, and I'm here to teach you . . ." says Rainbow.

Okay, it's a hot-for-hippy-teacher thing. I'm all over it. I breathe easy.

"Do you know what tantric sex is?" Rainbow asks.

I could dish some semicoherent gobbledygook about ancient mystic

Asian sex, but she wants me to be the blissfully ignorant manmoon-child, so naturally I turn myself into whatever she wants me to be. That's my job.

"No, I don't . . ."

Rainbow hands me a smile, and leads me through a translucent tie-dye cloth door into a bed with a room around it. It's the biggest bed I've ever seen. Overhead, high in the tall pointed ceiling is a skylight, where incense curls up thick from fat Buddha bellies; candles toss soft little drops of light everywhere; elephantheaded Indian gods with massive genitalia copulate with lionheaded goddesses; statue women stare with dozens of breasts; a halfman, halfbull is inside a godhead with a doghead; Japanese paintings of Jade-looking beautybabies intercourse in every position imaginable, one leg up over an ear, the other wrapped around a head; Old French postcards of cherubinesque honeys are Frenched and doggied; a guy goes down (or would that be up?) on himself; and a shrine of rosebudvaginas and phalluspeni smiles. Pillows and cushions plump, velvety; blankets, fur, and fat cloth make me feel like a cat, and I want to roll around getting my belly stroked while nubile handmaidens feed me catnip.

A sculpture of a vagina starts talking to me: "Hi, David, welcome to the party, come on in."

And in the center of it all a big picture of a dark man with long black curly hair and brown magnets for eyes that keeps staring at me no matter where I go in the room, it's freaky. He's hard and soft at the same time. I've never seen the guy, but he looks familiar, like he's the kind of guy who could set you straight if you're floundering around. And I'm so very full of flounder presently. I make a mental note to find a wise, kind, benevolent guru teacher as soon as I leave Rainbow's. I'm still looking.

"That's Baba Ram Wammalammadingdong," says Rainbow.

I'm sure she didn't really say that, but that's what it sounds like to my seventeen-year-old man child idiot ears, all Dr. Seussy.

"He's the master of sensual enlightenment."

That's what I wanna be when I grow up: Master of Sensual Enlightenment.

"Sexual transcendance can only happen when you are connected to the life force that flows through all living things," breathes Rainbow. "You have to open, I mean really open, all of your . . . shock absorbers."

Years later I will realize it was my chakras and not my shock absorbers that need opening, but at the time I couldn't care less. I'll open my shock absorbers, my athletic supporters, my cookie jar, whatever she wants. I just need to get paid, and I need to get paid now. I'm seeking enlightenment through cold hard cash.

"Why don't we start by meditating?"

Rainbow settles into a big comfy-womfy cushy cushion crosslegged and motions for me to do the same.

I balk. I'm naturally curious by nature, I'm very interested in the whole third-eye transcendent-sex thing, and picking up some exotic kinky eastern sex tips would be grand, but I have GOT to get my money up front.

I sigh quiet. I know for a fact it will not help us achieve harmony with the life force that flows through all living things if I tell Rainbow she needs to pay me now.

I am dreadfully dithered.

But just when things are looking their most dodgy, the gods smile upon me, and Rainbow, God love her, knows what I need and cannot ask for.

"Oh, shit, you need some bread, don't you?" she says.

I could've cried. I see this as a clearcut sign that I'm being taken care of by something bigger than myself.

Rainbow gets out of crosslegged, rummages through an old macramé bag, and returns with four skanky twenties, a nasty ten, a funky five, four filthy ones and a bunch of loose change, then hands me the whole kitandkaboodle.

I'm starting to dig this crazy chick. I can see her scrimping and saving to give herself a treat. Me. I'm the treat for my trick. I vow then and there to be a pot of gold for this Rainbow.

X X X

ANNE FRANK'S father is the only role that absolutely must be played by a boy. So by virtue of the fact that I show up, I become Mr. Frank. And in the instant I'm handed that role, I become, for better and for worse, an actor.

I enjoy being Mr. Frank. But being surrounded by all those gorgeous, popular, really nice-smelling Texas beauties is delicious. And much to my amazement, they all seem to like me now.

In the scene, Mr. Frank's supposed to celebrate. During rehearsals Teacher keeps telling me to celebrate more, but I don't know how. We don't do much celebrating where I come from. The night before our performance I'm watching television. Hershel Bernardi does some crazy Greek dance where he throws his hands up in the air and shakes his booty. The lightbulb goes off over my head.

This is how Mr. Frank is gonna celebrate.

X X X

"OPENING THE gate that leads to the garden of earthly delights can only be achieved through a woman's pleasure."

Rainbow pauses to make sure I got it.

"Opening the gate that leads to the garden of earthly delights can only be achieved through a woman's pleasure."

She looks at me intensely, so I understand how important this is.

So I think about it hard. It's comforting to have someone telling me what to think about. I don't have to make any decisions, and right now, decisions are just disasters waiting to happen.

Garden of earthly delights. A woman's pleasure. A woman's orgasm. Tumblers click in my head, a lock snaps open, and I see the light. A woman's pleasure is the key to sexual ecstasy. Now that I have my money, I'm keenly interested in this whole thing.

"A man can have multiple orgasms . . . most people don't know that, but it's true. And I can show you how to do it." Rainbow says with absolute conviction.

Multiple orgasms? Hell, I have one and it nearly kills me. But I'm crazy curious to see if I can incorporate some clitoris into my penis.

"There's a line where your orgasm is, it's kinda like a waterfall. See, it's like you're in a beautiful warm river, and the current is pulling you along, and you're headed towards the waterfall, you're getting closer and closer . . . until you're hanging right there on the edge of the waterfall, but you're not letting yourself go over. You just get inside your own orgasm, and you can stay there as long as you want, as long as you don't release. Do you know what release means?"

Yeah, I think I got the idea.

"No, what do you mean?" I ask.

"Your release is your ejaculation. So you can orgasm without ejaculating," Rainbow says carefully.

And the weird thing is, I know exactly what she means. River, waterfalls, release, the whole shebang.

"I know it sounds totally . . . far out . . . but if you can wrap your cosmic mind around this, you'll always have lots of groovy lovemaking in your life. You probably won't get it tonight, but it's something you can always practice. By yourself, with a partner, doesn't matter. In the words of Baba Ram Wammalammadingdong, 'Practice makes perfect.'"

I'm starting to really like this Wammalammadingdong guy.

X X X

ALL EYES upon me, during our dramatic presentation of *The Diary of Anne Frank*, I do my crazy Greek dance, throwing my hands up in the air and shaking my booty. Well, the roof tears off the sucker, and that *Music Man* feeling lights me up like the Fourth of July on Christmas morning.

Somehow I've managed to transform the heartbreaking tragedy of the Franks into a showcase for my comedy stylings.

That moment turns me from an odd-duck newcomer into a dashing ladies' boy.

And I owe it all to Anne Frank, martyr and symbol of all that is good in human beings.

✕ ✕ ✕

"WOW, THAT sounds . . . far out." I've never said "far out" before or since, but Rainbow eats it up like wavy gravy with a tie-dye spoon.

She takes off her robe. She's the only industrial sex customer I ever have who takes off her clothes while I still have mine on. And for an old broad (again with the proviso that anyone over the age of twenty-five years is Old) she's got a riproaring body. Supple muscles firm lithe and graceful, breasts slung low, with big brown chocolate-kiss nipples in the middle. Mental note to self: as far as books go, don't judge them by their covers.

Rainbow seems to be one of those rare people who's actually comfortable with her own naked body.

"You have a beautiful body . . ." I would've said it whether it was true or not, but in this case it is true, which does makes it easier.

She likes it. She's not desperate like Georgia or Frannie, but she likes it.

"Do whatever makes you happy," says Rainbow.

"Do you want me to take my clothes off?" Just trying to keep the customer satisfied.

Wow. Whatever makes me happy. Reminds me of my mom. No one says that to me in real life, never mind when I'm chickening.

Seems like if you're gonna learn to orgasm without ejaculating, you should be naked. So I take off my clothes. Rainbow sits opposite me crosslegged on that continent of a bed. I try, but I just can't get the crosslegged thing going. My pedophile grandfather's coalminer soccerplaying legs are just too unyielding. I'm tugging and pulling, cuz I'm trying to suck it up and play through the pain, but damn, this shit hurts.

"Don't do it if it hurts. Don't do anything that hurts . . ." Rainbow flows. You gotta hand it to the hippies, when it comes to peace and love and all that business, they really know their shit.

Rainbow shows me how to deepbreathe, and we deepbreathe until we feel the life force flowing through us. I don't actually feel the life force flowing through me as such, but she does, and that's good enough for me. The crumpled bills in my pocket are filling me with the life force.

Rainbow and I Ohhhhhhhhhhhhhhmmmmm for about a fortnight. Eventually I do feel a little lightheaded, like when I first smoked a cigarette. But hey, if she wants to pay me to breathe and say om, that's rolling off a log for a chicken.

Finally when Rainbow is om'd out, she takes my hand, places it on her breast, looks me in the eyes, and with a hypnotic smile shows me how to roll that mammoth mammarian poolcue tip between my thumb and forefinger, and it gets bigger and tighter, until it feels like it's ready to pop, while she makes airsuck sounds of pleasure.

I can smell her now, Rainbowing as she makes my hand the axis between her legs around which she gyrates, nestling my head into her neck and whispering, "Kiss me soft . . ."

I eat her neck like a fruitcake while she revs in growly moans, everything moving in rhythm like a well-oiled sex machine, the fur blanket softly soft as she guides me like an air traffic controller. Then Rainbow replaces my hand with my mouth and she huffs and she puffs like she's gonna blow the house down, jimjamming and earthquakeshaking.

I smile inside. I'm getting a crash course in the fine art of a woman's orgasm, and I'm getting paid for it. America—what a country!

"Now I'm right there," she pants, ". . . if I let myself, I'd go right over the waterfall . . . but . . . I'm . . . not . . . I'm gonna stay . . . right here and let the . . . waves roll through me . . . there's one . . . slow down . . . Stop!" Rainbow squeezes, fists clenching and unclenching like a baby breastfeeding, ". . . now slow . . . there's another one . . . ohhhhhhhhhhh-hhhhhhhhhhhhhhhhhhhhhh . . . God . . ."

Rainbow lets rip with a top-of-the-lungs scream. A gigantic little death. When she collapses at the tip of my tongue, I understand for the first time what they're talking about, as time warps, Einstein smiling somewhere, eternity in a second, infinity in a grain of sand.

I think of busting my ass in the grease of HFC. I think of my father slaving away at the explosives plant. I think about my grandfather shovelling coal down the mine. I sure as hell won't be getting black lung disease from this.

✗ ✗ ✗

ALABAMA IS ranked 50th in the nation in education when I'm eleven. My mom becomes so desperate she decides to enroll me and my brother in the best school in Alabama. The oxymoronicality of this is lost on no one. The only rub is that we have to pass the extremely rigorous entrance exam. My folks promise that if we pass the test, we can have some cool thing of our choice. My brother wants a wide handlebar bananaseat Stingray, the coolest bike on the planet. I want a brand new set of golf clubs. I like how shiny they look in the sporting goods store.

Tense anticipation grips our house in the days leading up to The

Test. Are we good enough to rub elbows with the crème de la crème of Hueytown, America?

The extremely rigorous test takes all day. It's rough terrain and grueling, but we've been trained well. Not just in facts and figures, but in succeeding American style, while failure breathes hot on your neck and those around you wither. It takes a week to get the results back. Longest week of my life.

We pass the test. There is much rejoicing.

Sadly my dad gets transferred, so we can't attend the best school in Alabama. But my mom and dad make good. They get my brother his cool wide-handlebarred Stingray with the big bananaseat, and they get me my shiny new golf clubs.

X X X

RAINBOW SLOWLY descends from Orgasm Mountain, while I stand next to her, nakedly rolling my big huge rock up my big huge hill.

After a brief intermission, Act II begins. She pulls me into the river, takes me right to the edge of the waterfalls, and then stops. The most important thing, she says, is to turn off your mind, and move into your body. You can't think and swim at the same time.

Once a man plunges over the waterfalls in his barrel, of course, it's all over for him. For a while at least. So you have to be very careful and really pay attention. I practice getting right on the edge and just sticking there. And it's good. When she does something particularly compelling, I feel the spray in my face and the pull of the fall, and by God, quivers do quiver me, then I quickly pull myself back.

Rainbow's my Seeingeye sexdog.

"Wow, that was groovy . . ." I say, when it's clear we're done.

Groovy? I can't believe that came out of my mouth, but as usual I've ceased to exist in my need to please.

I don't know what to do now. Should I hang out? Are we friends? I think for a minute. I still don't feel that creeping mudslide of depression I always get after I chicken. I'm just a little confused, that's all. But looking around, I can see myself moving right in here and being the sextoy for all of Rainbow's old greatbodied freakyhippie chicks. Sounds like fun, I think, as I grab at another salvation flotation device.

"I have something for you . . ." Rainbow's sweet as you please, slipping on an old soft tie-dye robe. I follow at her heels like a naked chicken-puppy. She reaches in a drawer and I'm expecting a nice fat juicy tip. Twenty, maybe fifty. Instead Rainbow pulls out a feather.

A feather.

"It's an earring," says Rainbow.

I have to work hard not to show how totally disgusted I am as I take out the rhinestone in my ear and replace it with the feather. I look in the mirror. To my amazement, I actually like the way it looks. Kind of tribal. Even though I silently scoff when she presents it to me, that feather becomes a war souvenir, and I wear it on and off for many years.

And whenever I do, I think of Rainbow.

She kisses me on both cheeks. She thanks me. I thank her. She doesn't say we should get together again soon, or that we should stay in touch. I love that. I did what I came to do, we both got what we wanted, and that, as they say, is that.

Rainbow's the only trick I ever had who gave me more than I gave her.

Motorcycling away from Rainbow, floating on my feather earring in the sweetness of the cool Laurel Canyon night, I'm high on Rainbow's free love.

That she paid for.

If having sex for money were always this good, I'd still be an industrial sex technician.

11

I LOVE YOU MOMMY

And sex and sex and sex and sex . . . I'm shattered! — The Rolling Stones

X X X

THE BEGINNING of the end comes innocently enough. Just a normal job on a normal day in the life of a normal seventeen-year-old boy hooker. Tooling through a trendy treed Pacific Palisades neighborhood chocabloc with brown migrant workers mowing green lawns, pink children throwing red balls, and white women driving overpriced foreign automobiles, I have that wonderful sense of déjà vu all over again as I go from the seedy pit of Hollywood to the clean hightone America of my youth.

I ring the bell. Split a second and that's how long it takes a postmodern June Cleaver to pull the door open too fast, say Hello too hard, and lead me into her too-immaculate, too-decorated home.

She does look good for an old broad, except for all the cakey makeup. Brownish hair slicked back anorexic-ballerina style, eyes drowning in pools of blue eye shadow, she's working a creamy calf-length sleeveless dress, plain white flats, and pearls. God love her, she put the pearls on for her chicken.

The kitchen's full of wallpaper choking on flowers. Linoleum rides the floor, Wedgwood watches from running boards, and a desert island sits arid with a butcherblock cuttingboard sinking in its middle. It's like a movie set of a perfect American home, with a housewife played by an actress who looks right for the role but is just a little too stiff.

"Did anyone see you come in?" There's a disturbing urgency in the lines fraying around the edges of her eyes and the veins popping on her neck.

Then she realizes how harsh she sounded, and tries to pretend she's all casual and carefree. "Not that it matters, but you know how people talk."

This bundle of too-tightly-tied wires tries to smile. But there's no smile there. Her pupils start darting back and forth like someone who's about to flunk a lie-detector test.

"And if anyone asks, maybe you could say you're a high-school student who's here to help me organize my miniatures. I collect miniatures. Would you like to see them?"

My Spidersenses are tingling, but my pokerface is firmly in place. Maybe she's just a little nervous. Family's out of town, looking for a little fun. Maybe she's never had sex with anyone besides her painintheassbastard husband. Maybe she just wants me to get nekked and tell her how hot she is.

Maybe.

X X X

THIS HOME movie's in the backyard, and you can practically hear the green of the grass and smell the birdies chirrupping. I'm six. My mom stands twenty feet in front of me holding a baseball. My bat is in the cocked-and-ready position, and I'm pure intention, staring that ball down. When Mom lobs in the ball, my eyes get big and hungry, like a lion spotting a sick wildebeest.

I attack the ball with a vicious compact swing, and when my bat whacks it square on the sweet G-spot, that ball flies like a human cannonball out of frame.

I drop the bat and my little legs churn me hard to first, whip me around second, fly me by third, flushed and radiant. I slide.

I'm safe at home.

X X X

"I'M SURE people have better things to do than stare at my back door. But let's say they were walking the dog, people like to walk their dogs, well I suppose they have to, but the point is they could see you and if they did, I just want us to be on the same page, you see what I mean?"

I follow my seven o'clock Monday trick to the Miniature Room, and as she finishes her monologue she opens a door revealing a room exploding with teeny tiny miniatures: little geldings with no little balls; tiny Chinese potentates and French diplomats; gnomes, sprites, and fairies; a very small Dorothy Gail from Kansas with her itty-bitty ruby slippers and her wee dog Toto; diminutive Bob's Big Boy, the Michelin Man, and the Sta-Puft Marshmallow Man; minute Benjamin Franklin, Ghengis Khan and even a mini-Marilyn Monroe, trying to hold her skirt down while the wind threatens to expose her panties for all eternity.

"Marilyn . . . now there was a woman."

SEXY's sick slick baritone rattles my bones and makes my soul moan and groan.

My seven o'clock Monday trick tries to smile again. She comes a little closer this time, but still hasn't hit it.

Her failure brings me back to the here and now though. She wants me to admire her miniatures. This is what I must do.

"Wow . . . this is really . . . incredible."

I say incredible like it's a good thing, whereas I mean incredible like it's a very scary thing. Everything's all lined up too perfectly, there's too much of it, and it's way too small. The whole thing makes me want to run, not walk, as fast as I can away from this woman.

But I don't. I can't.

"Thank you very much, it's taken a long time to collect, as you can imagine, and I'm . . ."

Her mouth is open, but nothing's coming out of this pearly woman standing in front of her collection of three-inch animals, movie characters, and famous historical figures.

Rule #8: If something seems weird it probably is.

But I can't listen to that voice inside of me that's never wrong.

I don't know how yet.

X X X

A CRICKETER with an excellent googly ball and superb English footballer with a real nose for goal was my dad. But he took up a whole new game he knew nothing about, just so he could play baseball with his American son.

The rhythm of playing catch is so soothing, the leathery smell, the hard of the ball, the red raised stitches, the pounding into the mitt, throwing to a perfect point, learning to make it dip, spin and curve.

Baseball's the only language my dad can speak with me, but he speaks it well.

The better I play the more he seems to love me, so I practice and practice, trying to be the most lovable American boy ever.

X X X

"THESE MINIATURES are totally amazing."

I'm desperately trying to resuscitate my pearly Mommy trick, who stares at me, a plaster of Paris mask of a normal person fixed on her face. I don't know what to do. But I'm 100 percent sure I gotta do something. Try to start the sex? I'm afraid if I touch her she'll shatter into a million pieces. And where's my stinking money? This is getting ridiculous. I'm gonna have to talk to Mr. Hartley about this shit, cuz I need my money in plain sight when I walk in the door, no questions asked.

"And they're so . . . small . . ." I say, trying desperately to fill in the Silence.

As soon as she hears the word "small" Mommy comes back to life, like some perfect robot replica of a human that gets activated by flipping a switch on the back of her head.

"Yes, they're so small, aren't they? I love how small they all are. I'll show you my favorite," she says.

I still don't know her name, or what the hell she wants, and I still DO NOT HAVE MY MONEY UP FRONT. But at least she's not acting like the walking dead anymore. She picks up a miniature with a rose complexion and dark hair, dressed very Civil War. Vaguely resembles Scarlett O'Hara.

"It's Scarlett O'Hara. Don't you just love her?" She stares rapturously at the lifeless Scarlett O'Hara doll like it's a three-inch lover.

"Yeah, I loved how she made that dress out of the curtains . . ." Having noticed that the mini-Scarlett's wearing the curtaindress, I feel this might help move us along.

"Oh gosh," she says, "I love that scene where Mammy sews the dress, and she grumbles the whole time. Oh that Mammy, she's such a character . . . and Scarlet puts on the dress, and of course she looks fabulous, and she goes to see Rhett in prison, and pretends like everything's okay, but he sees right through her. Oh that Rhett, he's such a scalliwag . . . and does he give her a tongue lashing. See the thing people don't realize is that they were always madly in love with each other, but never at the same time . . ."

And with that she clicks into some other time zone where crazed assassins lurk in every church tower, puts the little Scarlett carefully back in its place between President Abraham Lincoln and General Robert E. Lee, and ushers me out post haste.

Suddenly the forecast has gone from mostly sunny to severe storm warnings. Her skeletal structure visibly stiffens, skin tightening and lips constricting. For a second I think it's me. I see her on the phone with Mr. Hartley, who calls Sunny, who chucks me back in the dumpster.

I need my money.

I need my money.

I need my money.

x x x

BOYWONDER BASEBALL player is my next role. In all my team photos, with those rows of hopeful, glum, big-eared, goofy, shy, uncertain, vacant lads, I'm always on the bottom row, kneeling, smiling peacefully, like a little ballplaying boy buddah.

I play on All-Star teams with all the best players. The All-Star pictures are different than the average, every-day team photos. The All-Stars are cocksure, aggressive, and cunning, while the regular teams are more about being fat or uncomfortable or not quite sure what you're there for.

Being an All-Star Little Leaguer is excellent chicken training: the same performing adrenaline rush, the same illusion that attention equals love. Reminds me of Sunny's team of chickens. Only those players end up arrested, addicted, or dead, instead of on the cover of a Wheaties box.

x x x

MOMMY MUTTERS underbreath as I pad down the hall after her. The only words I can make out are, "ashamed," "irresponsible," and "neglect." I'm sure I'm not supposed to respond. In fact I'm sure she's not even aware she's vocalizing at this almost intelligible level.

She stops, turns suddenly, and tries to smile again. Again she fails. She looks down, regroups, and looks towards me, but not at me.

"My husband is not . . . with us . . ."

Euphemism for dead, I'm assuming, although for all I know he could be away on a golf junket.

"I thought you should know. I mean, I didn't want you to think . . ."

Who the hell cares what I think? I'm the whore houseboy, remember? And she doesn't want me to think what? That she's immoral? Unfaithful? Or just out of her mind?

"He took his own life. After our son died . . ."

"Oh . . . I'm really . . . sorry." My affable mask melts and I'm drenched in sad.

"We had a wonderful marriage. He was very handsome and attentive. My therapist said I should date again, that it would help me . . . get over the whole thing, so . . ."

I doubt this is the kind of date he had in mind.

"Everyone says I should sell the house, but I don't want to sell the house. I love this house . . . Would you sell the house?"

Now she's asking the boy hooker for real estate advice. "No, I think it's a great house. I thought that when I came in—I thought, 'This is a great house.'"

"It is, isn't it? That's what I'm gonna tell people. I'll just say, 'It's a great house . . .' My husband loved this house. He took his own life, did I tell you that?"

Yes, you did mention that.

"You'll have to forgive me, I've been very . . . forgetful lately. The fact is, he really never got over Braddy's passing. Braddy was our son . . . our only child. It was a terrible tragedy . . . his friend had been drinking . . . Braddy wasn't drinking, the coroner confirmed that. He had no alcohol in his system, or very little alcohol. They ran head-on into a bus . . . just like that . . . alive one second, dead the next. Makes you wonder, doesn't it?"

Yes, it certainly does.

"Yes, it certainly does," I say.

She looks at me like she's coming out of a coma, and for the first time I see who she was before all this shit happened: a beautiful wifemommy living large with the handsome husband, the cute kid, and the great house. Like my mom.

"You'll have to excuse me . . . I, uh, haven't been myself lately . . ."

Dead son. Husband offs himself. I want to take her in my arms, rock hurt right out of her and tell her everything's gonna be okay.

But I can't. I don't know how yet.

A sincere, "I'm sorry" is all I can muster.

What a couple of funked-up ducks we are, this ex-mom-slash-ex-wife and I, trying to get some love in the worst way.

"Thanks," she says.

She tries to smile again and this time it actually works. And when the smile finally does arrive it's very sweet, and drenched in sorrow, like cherries jubilee just about to be lit on fire.

X X X

LITTLE LEAGUE game tonight. I'm ten. I love playing, love being an All-Star. But as much as I love baseball games, I love night games best of all, because I get to play under the lights. Makes me feel like I'm half a step from Yankee Stadium, playing with Yogi, Mick, and the Moose.

But the afternoon sky looks like an old bruise, and a bullwhip wind whips into the flesh of the earth. I keep sneaking peeks outside, and every time I do my little heart sinks like a grape in warm jello.

Still, I slip on my white sanitary socks, slide my little blue stirrups over them, then my gray flannel pantaloons with blue pipes up the side, my blue-sleeved undershirt, gray uniform top with blue PIRATES on the front, then pull on my blue cap with P in the middle, and yank on my black cleats.

I rub mink oil lovingly into my glove, leather scratch-and-sniffing all over me, the glove molding further into the shape of my hand.

At six o'clock my mom asks my dad if maybe he shouldn't take me to the game, what with the storm and all.

He doesn't answer her. He gets in the car, I get in with him, and he starts driving me to my game.

x x x

BOY!

Screams the room Mommy leads me into: pennants, trophies, posters of ballplayers, old caramel colored baseball mitt with scuffed ball sitting in it, pictures of a brown-haired dimply boy growing up cute: grade school, Little League team, camp friends, high-school-tuxed, and posing with a pretty young polyester-plaid baby. There's a trophy exactly like one I had, it's so cool, it's just like my room.

But the longer I stand there the more wigged I get. We definitely have something in the woodshed here. This isn't a boy's room anymore. It's a museum of a boy's room. This room is dead.

"This is Braddy's room. His real name was Bradley, but when he was a baby he could only say Braddy and I guess it just stuck. He wanted to go to UCLA; that was his dream. And he was a very good athlete. Golf, tennis, baseball. Are you an athlete?" she asks with great expectations.

Doesn't take a rocket surgeon to figure out the answer to that one.

"Yes, I am."

"It was his friend Aaron . . . I never liked that boy; he was a very bad influence. I tried to tell Braddy, but he was stubborn, just like his dad. There was no alcohol found in Braddy. Or very little alcohol . . . very little alcohol . . ."

I want to get out of this dead boy's room.

I want to get paid.

I want.

"Would you . . . do me a favor?" she's filled with hesitation.

I still don't think she fully understands the nature of our transaction. That's what I'm here for. She give me money. I do her favors.

At first of course she has to give me MONEY!

"Sure," I say.

"Uh . . . would you mind . . . uh . . . putting these on?"

Pearly Mommy pulls a Hawaiian shirt and khaki shorts from the closet. I see Braddy behind her on the wall in a blown-up framed picture, dressed in the same Hawaiian shirt and khaki shorts.

"This was his favorite outfit. We used to kid him that it was his uniform. I washed it and washed it afterwards to get all . . . you know . . . the stains out. It wasn't easy, believe you me, but I've always said if you want something bad enough and you're willing to work at it, you can accomplish anything. Don't you think?"

"Definitely . . ." I manage to mumble.

Mommy hands me Braddy's Hawaiian shirt and khaki shorts.

"You don't mind do you?"

No, no, no, I can't, let's have a cup of tea or something and talk about getting you some professional help.

"No problem, that's cool . . ."

"Cool? Isn't that marvelous? That was Braddy's favorite word. He had a wonderful vocabulary, but every other word out of his mouth was "Cool." I'm just gonna go freshen up while you change. Would you like some cookies and milk?" she asks, like Oedipus's mother in pearls.

"Cookies and milk? Cool." I'm laying it on thick, but trying not to milk the cookies too hard.

She giggles like a crazy forty-year-old schoolgirl and leaves me alone in her dead son's room.

A Civil War rages in my head. The North says put on the outfit, then get the money. The South says get the money, then put on the outfit. After several bloody skirmishes the South relents, and I put on the outfit. But if she doesn't come back in with my money, that's it, I don't give a damn, I am going going gone.

The clothes fit like they were made for me. I look in the mirror. I look at Braddy in the khakis and Hawaiian shirt. Then I look back in the mirror.

I have completely disappeared.

X X X

THE SECOND my dad and I get to George Wallace Stadium, the heavens split and spit forth a furious wet rage, raindrops the size of manhole covers, hailstones the size of baseballs, Zeus and Thor putting on a celestial heavymetal thunderlightshow that rocks the house.

So we turn right around and head back home, rain thrashing the roof, windshield, and hood as a black funnel gyroscopes towards us up George Wallace Drive.

I'm terribly impressed by all this weather. I'm not scared. My dad's driving, and he knows exactly what he's doing.

The sleet sheets down so heavy now we can't see two feet in front of us, and the twister whirls dervishly straight at us.

But my dad never stops. All the other drivers pull their cars over to the side of the road, but not my old man. He doesn't say anything and neither do I, but I'm awed by the squall as we crawl home through the tempest.

The next day, in the calm after the storm, when I look across the street at the house that sits up high on the hill, I see the twister has torn the roof clean off.

And my dad drove me through all of it so I could play in a game that didn't even happen.

X X X

A FLIMSY blue negligee trimmed with black fox fur and red high heels walks through the door carrying a purple plate of brown cookies and a white glass of milk. Slimmy hips, pale belly, good gams nicely turned. Normally a sight like this would make my mojo corkscrew, but here, now, my heart plummets like the cable snapped, and I plunge fast, knowing there's a nasty crash coming and there's absolutely nothing I can do about it. Fevered hotsweats flash all over me, but I'm trying to keep this blank smile on my face, all the while wanting to scream, "Are you mad, woman? Go put some clothes on and check yourself into a clinic, where you can get some state-of-the-art mental health care!"

But I don't. I can't.

"My husband gave me this and I never got a chance to wear it. Do you like it?"

My mommy trick strikes what's supposed to be a tarty pose, but ends up looking more like a mental patient than a sex baby.

"Have a cookie . . ."

She moves the plate of cookies towards me, and there it sits, half-hidden under a cookie like an invitation to the gold miner's ball: my envelope.

Casually, oh-so-casually, I pick up the cookie over my envelope, take a bite out of it, then palm the sweet succor of my money into the back pocket of the dead Braddy's khaki's. I'm a hundred bucks richer and suddenly I don't give a whatever about nothing. And the cookie's good. Moist. I like a moist cookie. I wash it down with the milk.

Envelope in hot pocket, cookie in cool belly, and devilmaycare upon my lips, I squint my eyes, and make her into the hottyhot porno star baby of my loverstudguy movie.

"Why don't you come over and sit on the bed with Mommy, Braddy? You don't mind if I call you Braddy, do you?" She smiles like Mother Mary on acid from the bed covered by the blanket with the sports guys on it.

No, no, no, no, no, no.

"No," I say, "that's cool."

✗ ✗ ✗

SATURDAY AFTERNOON when I'm ten I come home from playing ball, and the house is empty. This is unusual. My mother's home. I don't know how I know this, but I know it all the same. I call her name. She doesn't answer. I have a panic. Has she gotten sick of us, sick of Hueytown, sick of America, sick of her punishing husband? Worst of all, sick of me?

I check the house, my little heart pounding. She's gone. I know it. It never dawned on me that Mother might decide to bolt.

Breathing harder I flopsweat into my parent's bedroom. She's not there. I go into the closet, where all the big pants and huge dresses live. The closet potpourri envelopes me: mothballs, shoe polish and fresh laundry dancing together.

When I found her in there one time crying, it had seemed so odd and horrible. But now I'm actually hoping she's in there crying.

She's not.

I quicksand further into fear, and the more I squirm with the thought that she's gone, the faster I sink.

✗ ✗ ✗

MY TRICK mommy pats the bed next to her, the cue for Braddy to sit on the dead bed with his bereaved mother. Is it too late to give back the envelope and get the hell out? Yes, I believe it is. Just do what she wants and everything'll be fine, you'll get some ice cream, have a hang in 3D, and see if Sunny's got some sweet young baby for you to swing with.

When I sit on the bed, Mommy pulls me into her and starts rocking. I'm confused. Does she want me to get sexy with her? Does she want me to be her little boy? I can barely breathe, suffocated by all this Mommy, her sickly sweet perfume pounding on my temples.

She lays back on Braddy's bed and takes me with her. I end up embryonic, head on her chest. Then she guides my mouth to her breast, and it's clear dear dead Braddy is supposed to suckle on Mommy.

So I suck.

Mommy guides me up on top of her, between her legs, and her hips stiltingly do a spasmodic grind while she fumbles with my zipper.

I fish myself out. Fish being the operative word. As in cold and limp. Again, there are many things in life you can fake, and erection is not one of them. My eyes are clamped, because I don't want to see what's underneath me. So I position myself where I can get maximum rubbage, and with my eyes closed, I find the loverstudguy voice in my head:

"Oh baby . . . give it to me you nasty little baby . . . you love it, don't you, baby? Oh baby, baby, baby."

That gets the blood moving in the right direction, and suddenly I'm in, thank you Jesus! And once I'm in, I'm in.

"Do you love Mommy, Braddy?"

She grabs my head and puts me right in her face.

It jolts me right out of my river, and lands me smackdab in the middle of this dead boy inside his mommy, who's got wet eyes I didn't even notice were crying, as she downloads her pain right into me.

I need to scream. I don't. I can't.

"I . . . I do . . . I lo- . . . I lo- . . . lo . . ."

The words just won't come out no matter how much I push them.

"Do you love Mommy, Braddy?"

She asks again, voice cracking like a pane of dropped glass, wild eyes pleading with her dead son while she has sex with her boy whore.

Braddy's supposed to tell Mommy he loves her, but I can't get the words out of my mouth.

Until the need to please takes over.

"I love you, Mommy" somehow burbles out between my frozen lips.

She grabs my hips and starts pulling me into her heart.

So I shut my eyes, and in the dark I manage to get everything working again, and she starts making little sex sounds, so I'm thinking I'm earning my money at least.

Her body lurches, and I open my eyes just in time to see her lean her head over the side of the bed and unload a stream of sick onto the floor, the wave of vomit smell breaking all over me.

She pushes me off her like a mom lifting an automobile off her child who's trapped under the front tire. Then she bolts out of bed and out the door.

I sit on the edge of the dead Braddy's bed, Mommy's secretions shining on me, and the smell of her sick cutting through me.

X X X

FRANTIC AS only a ten-year-old boy can be, I bounce out of the closet, down the hall, and through the back door. A huge acutely sloping back yard is behind the Alabama house. It could've been a ski jump if it ever snowed in Hueytown. Which of course it never did.

I glide the sliding glass door open, and run into the back yard. It's hot outside. You never realize in Alabama how cool the air conditioning is inside until you step out into the inferno. Just walking out of the house I sweat, my blood pounding. I stand stock still. Listen. I hear her. Crying. I can't see her yet, but I can hear her, and I'm comforted by the company of her misery.

My mother's leaning on a mammoth pine, sobbing in wet spasms. Next thing I know I'm holding her hand, and she's looking down at me, eyes deep swimming holes of sadness. I reach up hug high, and she wraps me in her arms, transfusing me with all that primal pain and absent love.

Gradually the swelling of my mom's sobs subsides, the tide rolls back
out, and we walk hand in hand into the house, talking about thisandthat,
nothing really, just easy talk.

My mom and I make cookies, the measuring, the beating, and the
sifting pure succor, the smell of chocolate vanilla and butter melting me
as it gets stronger and deeper, the treat of licking mixer blades, the raw
dough slices of paradise, waiting, waiting, waiting, for the first warm bite
to explode in my mouth, the ache buried once again beneath the silence.

X X X

CAREFUL NOT to step in the sick I step out of Braddy's dead bed and shed
his dead clothes and slip back into my own. I touch the hundred-dollar
bill. That's better. Normally I want my tip, and God knows I earned it,
but today I feel like a diver surfacing too fast, my insides bending, and if I
don't get out of here quick, I'm sure my brain's gonna explode.

I shoot like infected sperm out of Braddy's room. But I can't leave yet.
I have to make sure she's okay. I tiptoe down the hall, and peek in the
bedroom. It's long-day's-journey-into-night dark in there. I hear a little
mumbly snuffly sound.

"Uh . . . excuse me . . ." I say softly.

More mumbles and snuffles.

"Um . . . I was just wondering if you're . . . okay." Louder this time,
poking my head further into the room.

Mumbles. Snuffles.

"Do you need . . . are you all right?" I say so I know she'll hear me.

Her head snaps up.

"Do you want more money? Is that what you want? There's more
money on the desk in the den, take whatever you want, but please, just
go . . ." Her face is all puffy red mad like Lady Macbeth at the end when
she's trying to get that damn spot out.

It's like looking at a wounded animal bleeding in the middle of the road. You have to stop the car and get out and help. Don't you?

"Are you sure you don't want—"

"Just go! GO!"

Her shriek curdles my blood, and bolts me down the hall. But even now, I need my money. That's how empty I am. So I jam into the den, and open a fancy-looking box on the desk where a wad of cash stares at me. Gotta be five hundred bucks there. My first impulse is to clean her out. Hey, I earned it. But I can't. I take a fifty.

I feel like I earned it.

12

PEAS

&

CORNBREAD

Going down, sir! — Droopy Dog

I FINGER my pager. It's become my anti-talisman bad luck charm. I'm having a lot of trouble rolling that big huge rock up that big huge mountain this morning, sitting in Existentialism, trying to focus on Sister Tiffany and the meaning of life. Her mouth is moving, but unfortunately, I can't hear a word she's saying. Usually I spend quality Existentialism time staring at Kristy, dreaming about the sweet little life we're gonna have together.

Not today.

"Do you love Mommy, Braddy?"

That voice keeps ringing in the belltower of my head. I see myself in the Hawaiian shirt and khakis looking at myself in the mirror next to the picture of Braddy in the Hawaiian shirt and khakis. Dad blowing his brains out with a shotgun, Braddy all boozed up driving head-on into a bus, Mommy washing that shirt over and over until all her dead son's blood is gone.

"Do you love Mommy, Braddy?"

I thought about trying to call Kristy after I left the Palisades. I actually had the phone in my hand, but I couldn't pull the trigger. I felt like picking a fight. So I went out and bought my dayold birthday cake and my tub of ice cream, and I ate it all up. But still I felt hungry enough to have sex with a horse. I tried to sleep but that was a complete joke.

So I went to Sunny's. 3D was business as usual. The Dixie Chickens fighting and French kissing. Cruella and Sunny doing the Temptations. People I never saw before and would never see again. Jade was not in attendance. That was sad. Sunny hugged me, kissed me on both cheeks N'Awlins style, and tried to cop a feel.

"Hoo-ie boy, if you ain't a sight for sore eyes. How's the job tonight, baby? Uh-oh, one of them, huh? Well, lemme getcha some Jack and a Jill."

He got me a shot of Jack Daniels, then introduced me to a sweety looking girl he'd christened Buttercup. When she wandered into the restaurant that afternoon, Sunny'd sprinkled some magic fairy dust on her, and Poof! here she was in 3D, hanging out with a smoking bong, giggling with a gaggle of freaks. She could be thirteen, could be fifteen, but she's certainly no more than sixteen. She's medium-sized blondish cornfed gaptooth bangs-and-ponytail cute. She couldn't really keep up with the lightningfast 3D banter, but the girl now named Buttercup was totally adorable in her little Daisy Mae cutoffs, duffel bag and ruffly dorky mall shirt.

Sunny whispered that he wants me to break her in. She's my perk for doing a bang-up job. So after hanging a while I took her back to my hovel. Me, the one-boy sex factory, have never had a woman in my carpetwalled shithole. I don't wanna shit where I live.

Buttercup is essence of sweet, but there's definitely a FOR RENT sign in her eyes. Someone has clearly stuck a monkey wrench deep in Buttercup's gears. I wasn't sure whether she'd ever had sex, but Sunny put me in charge of making a chicken out of her, and I was taking my responsibility very seriously.

I was sure I was doing her a favor by transforming her from a no-skills runaway to a bread-winning chicken, getting her off the streets where she was sure to get the shit repeatedly kicked out of her.

I laid out the whole thing, soup to nuts, for the girl now named Buttercup. Guess what the first lesson was?

GET THE MONEY UP FRONT

After I briefed her on the ins and outs of independent sex contracting, we moved to the hands-on section of the tutorial. She was an enthusiastic student, and her learning curve steep, especially in her oral exam, which she passed with flying colors. More important, she had that eager-to-please, turned-off turned-on quality that can be very helpful in the making of a first-class whore. Plus, of course, she was dead broke, hungry, had no resources, no home, no family to take care of her, and nowhere in the whole world to go, which helps.

Then I was swimming in the river with the girl now named Buttercup, endorphin dolphins frolicking beside me, and when the spray of the waterfall hit my face everything seemed right with the world.

But here, now, the day after, in Existentialism class, I can't stop fingering my pager.

"Does Braddy love Mommmy?"

The top of my head feels like it's about to pop off.

Finally, mercifully, class is over, and I bolt fast. I hope Kristy's following me. I need Kristy to follow me. I decide if Kristy's following me, the gods are on my side. As I walk down the hill overlooking Hollywood onto the immaculate lawn, the air rejuvenates and the sun revives me. It's a clean day, cuz it's windy, and you can see all the way to the ocean. I deepbreathe, smell the warm grass, and wait for Kristy, trying to look like a normal Joe College guy enjoying his existential sundrenched afternoon, instead of a chicken on his day off waiting for a girl like his life depends upon it.

But there's no Kristy.

The gods hate me.

I'm used to craving the normal of her, but today the craving's consuming me. I realize now I need to take her out to lunch, talk about nuns, drink a few beers, maybe even have some old-fashioned American apple-pie sex. I wait and wait, barely able to contain myself, ants multiplying in my pants every second.

Finally, when I've stood all I can stand, I go hunting for Kristy. Back in class Sister Tiffany gabs with a few stragglers. I chainsaw down to the library. Nothing. Back to the lawn. Nothing. As I walk into the cafeteria, I bump into someone. My fist has a life of its own, and it clenches without authorization from upper management. Luckily I stop it before it can rise up in anger. Then my polite British schoolboy takes over, and I'm an apologizing machine, saying sorry so often the apologizee looks at me like I escaped from Bedlam. I turn off the sorry button, and scan the lunchroom. No Kristy, no Kristy, no Kristy. Jam back up the hill. Check the lawn. No Kristy. Some serious snark is clogging my pipes. I want to smash a mirror with a five-iron, crash my skull into a brick wall, smash my hand through a TV screen. If I don't find this girl I can't stand to be around for more than a night at a clip, I am seriously gonna do something very bad.

X X X

A WINNEBAGO trailer is hitched to the back of our faux-woodpaneled station wagon, and my mom and dad whisk us off to look for America. The Grand Canyon invites us into Mother Earth. Old Faithful is a holy explosion from the blowhole of the planet, one you can set your watch by. Glacial ice creeps down a mountain slower than time. We gather driftwood like old sailors' bones and make a bonfire where spirits of Chippewa shamans dance. We see bears, meeses, and now and then a beaver.

My mom and dad embrace America more fully than any born-and-bred Americans I've ever seen. They show us the nooks and crannies of warm sweet lakes, a Petrified Forest, and the Great White Way.

And I never thanked them for that.

X X X

A SHAFT of golden California sunlight spotlights Kristy, looking like Madonna, Mother of Jesus Christ our Lord and Savior. She's writing a note by my motorcycle.

Kristy, Kristy, Kristy!!!

I sneak up behind her and wrap my fingers around her eyes. After a flinch reflex she realizes it's me, and when she relaxes back into my arms, everything suddenly seems A-okay on this sunny day.

"Sister Tiffany?" says Kristy.

"You didn't tell anybody about us, did you?" I ask.

"Hell no," she says.

"You swear to God?" I ask.

"I swear to God, Sister—"

I spin Kristy around, and she's all shocked surprise—

"I mean, David, uhm . . . how's it hangin'?"

"So, you and Sister Tiffany?" I smile.

"You don't mind?" she bats eyelashes.

I always forget how funny Kristy is.

"No, I always wanted to have a three-way with a nun," I say. "Wanna go for a ride?"

"Where?"

"Your place."

I kiss her lips, which are once again not too thin at all.

"Are you serious?" she asks.

"Sure."

This is turning out so much better than I imagined.

"Well, I was supposed to go the library, but . . . okay, sure, why not . . ." she says, very Holly Golightly.

But again the gods toy with me, for just as I've finally forgotten all about it, my pager goes off.

X X X

MY IMMIGRANT father slurpsucks translucent fat globules off pickled pig's feet as my brother and sisters, and I take turns telling what great American things we did that day. I'm eight.

My six-year-old runty, logicdriven, towheaded, mathgenius brother loathes peas with a searing passion, and tonight he's decided he will eat no more of them. My mom speaks to him about his peas. He ignores her. Finally when she presses, he announces in a grown-up voice, "I'm not going to eat any more peas."

My mother makes a show of consternation, but you can tell her heart's not in it, and the whole thing's going to blow over in a moment.

Except a burr's in the bugger that's up my Dad's ass.

"Eat yer bluddy peas," spits my father.

This is odd. He never interferes with the raising of his children. So I assume my little brother will just cave and eat his peas.

To my shock and amazement, he stares my dad down.

This is getting fun.

X X X

MY PAGER going off sends shots of sex and fear and dread and money slamming into my solar plexus, and I snap shut without even being aware I'm snapping shut.

And I do it right in front of Kristy.

"Is everything all right?" she drags me back from my personal torture chamber.

"No, I'm fine. Sure, yeah . . . I'm fine, everything's fine."

But the more I say how fine everything is, the less fine it seems.

"Is there anything I can do?" Kristy's all genuine concern.

"No, it's a work thing. I gotta make a call . . ." I give her a thin gruel of a smile, trying to stay loose when I feel tighter than a bodybuilder's ass.

"You want me to come with you?" Kristy's full of care.

"No!" I barked harsh and loud. I want the word back even before it leaves my mouth.

Can we do a second take on that?

Kristy sighs. Suddenly I've gone from sweet boyfriend to harsh freak.

"David, what is it? What's the matter?" Kristy stands there and asks.

And I love her for that.

✗ ✗ ✗

SCARY SILENCE is back at the diningroom table, like in one of those Westerns when some feller accuses some other feller of cheatin' and everybody's waitin' fer the first gun to be drawn.

"Eat those bluddy peas or I'll stot summink off yer bluddy heed," my father barks.

Stot is bounce. Heed is head. Clearly he means business. But my runty brother will not be moved.

"You will sit in that bluddy chair 'til you finish those bluddy peas." My father's head reddens and his veins bulge as I picture myself loosening a valve on the back of his head and watching the steam blow out his ears like an old-fashioned cartoon workwhistle.

In slow motion my brother forks one pea, painfully places it in his mouth, and with strained face forces the poison pellet down his gullet.

Silence. More silence. Crazy straining silence.

After three more excruciating peas go down, everyone resumes their happy banter. Except my dad. He says nothing. I'm laughing my ass off inside. My little genius brother's twisting our father on his own rack.

X X X

"SORRY, MY boss, he's . . . got it in for me, he's been riding my ass. But I'm really sorry . . ."

I backpedal and shadowbox for all I'm worth.

"I'm confused. What do you . . . do exactly?"

"Deliveries . . . packages, envelopes, scripts, you know. I go to Malibu, or Beverly Hills, or the Valley, and if I work at night, or do emergency jobs, it's really good money. And since my parents cut me off, I gotta make money. It's a great job, except for my asshole boss . . ." I lean in confidentially. "He wants to, you know . . . seduce me."

"Oh my God, that's illegal. Do you want me to tell my dad, cuz he could maybe—"

Obviously I don't want Daddy in my beezwax.

"No, that's okay, I talked to the owner. He's on my side. And I don't wanna lose my job."

"Sure, absolutely. Well, I'm sorry. If there's anything I can do, just ask, okay?"

Just ask. The way she says it, it seems like the easiest thing in the world.

"Lemme go make this call, and . . . I'll be right back . . ." I move in now, all denial and survival. "And I'm really sorry. Will you forgive me?"

"Of course," says Kristy, "I'm just glad you felt you could trust me enough to tell me the truth."

"Yeah . . ." I nod.

I almost believe it all myself.

X X X

FURIOUSLY MY dad vents his spleen on the innocent plates and dishes, and even as I'm putting the last bit of roast beef in my mouth, he's snatching, jerking, and cleaning my plate. He flings knives and forks into the dishwater zing zing zing, wrestles with the pots and pans, cleansing and purging them faster than humanly possible, slamming them back into the cupboards twang bang clang. Then he roars off to the couch, rams on the big TV, and snores in a feverish rhythm.

Years later I'll read the Edgar Allan Poe story about a guy who kills some old codger, buries him under the house, then goes insane when he hears the dead man's heart pounding louder and louder, until he can't stand it any more and confesses to the cops.

It will remind me of my father's snores.

X X X

$200 JOB. Right now. Mr. Hartley wants to know if I can handle it.

"Absolutely, Mr. Hartley. I'm on it."

Mr. Hartley chuckles.

"Excellent. David, we've had great feedback, and your client from Saturday was very complimentary."

"I appreciate that, it means a lot to me . . . Thanks."

I'm genuine. I'm real. This is so rare for me right now. And I'm able to do it with my pimp easier than the girl I'm falling in love with.

"So I was curious what happened on Monday . . ."

I can hear the sinister pipe organ creeping in the background as Mr. Hartley switches gears all over me. My breath is gone. What did I do? What did I not do? What did she say? What kind of shit am I in now?

Does Braddy love Mommy?

"Uh . . . nothing. Why, did she say something?"

A vise squeezes my temples as I tremble.

"Why don't you tell me exactly what happened?" Mr. Hartley's a cagey bastard.

Say as little as possible. When in doubt say even less.

"Well . . . it was just a normal job, you know . . ."

I don't think I can say anything less than that.

"Did she seem . . . upset?"

If I say she wasn't upset he'll know I'm a liar. But if I say she was upset, then am I responsible for whatever bad shit came down in the wake of my home visit?

"Uh . . . yeah. I guess she was a little upset. But I didn't do anything, I swear to God . . ." I'm tapdancing as fast as I can, and Mr. Hartley feels me all the way from Immaculate Heart College to Sunset Strip.

"I'm not accusing you of anything. I just want you to tell me exactly what happened." Mr. Hartley's got his no-more-messing-around voice on.

I suppress a sigh of great weight.

"Well, yeah, she did seem upset. But it wasn't my fault, I swear to God. She even gave me a tip . . ." My voice suddenly sounds so scared and little and pitiful.

"David"—Mr. Hartley does that thing grownups do when they start a sentence with your name— "we're not accusing you of anything. That's why I gave you this job today, to let you know we're very pleased with your work. But I need to know what happened. Now think carefully."

"Well, to tell you the truth, she seemed kinda . . ."

I don't want to say the word, but I have a feeling he's gonna make me.

"She seemed kinda what?" asks Mr. Hartley.

"Well, kinda . . . crazy."

There. I said it.

Pause. Long pause.

"I don't want you talking to anybody about this. Nobody. Do you understand?" Mr. Hartley's dead-serious scares the shit outta me.

"Yes, absolutely. No, I mean, I never talk to anybody, about anything."
I pant frantically.

"The client had a . . . problem." Mr. Hartley's voice flatlines.

"What happened?" Sweat breaks out everywhere.

"The less you know the better."

The way Mr. Hartley says it, I know this part of the conversation is over, which is just fine with me, cuz I never want to think about this shit for the rest of my life.

So I swallow it all whole, and lock it in my pressure cooker, where it will feed on me until I can get rid of it.

While the whole in my bucket gets a little bigger.

"I might have something for you this weekend. I'm just waiting for a confirmation," Mr. Hartley's back to being buttah.

"Excellent. I'll make sure the pager's on vibrate."

Mr. Hartley's wry chuckle is highly gratifying.

He gives me the 411 while I disconnect from myself. Did Mommy slit her wrist in a bubblebath? Swallow a bottle of pills? Suck on an antique pistol? She seemed like the dramatic type.

Change the record, Braddy.

X X X

MY BROTHER sits at the dinner table 'til eleven o'clock that night, when he forces down his last poison pea. We're all supposed to be asleep of course, but it's much too exciting for that.

He looks so small as he opens our bedroom door, backlighted like a hero, one small boy standing tall against the Man. He smiles a funny little smile. I want to tell him how great he is, but already the silence has its hand around my throat.

"What time is it?"

I already know it's eleven.

"Eleven," he says.

"Did you get grounded?" I say.

"Not yet," he says.

He gets into bed. We lie there, not sleeping, co-conspirators in a rich secret rebellion. We don't have peas again for a long time.

✖ ✖ ✖

KRISTY'S WEIRDED out when I tell her I gotta go. But I kiss her goodbye with all the tender I can muster. Then I motorbike to a prestigious Beverly Hills Hotel for my two-hundred-dollar job. She's a big-boned sweet-faced executive from some Midwestern beefy beer-soaked wonderbread place who's in town for business, and heard from a girlfriend who's friends with Frannie about the service. About me. God love Frannie.

They weren't all freaks. I want to make that clear. I worked with a whole string of Midwestern ladies, with those nasal flat accents hard and thick as a brick.

Wonderbread wants to talk. About her painintheassbastard boss. Apparently she does all the work and he gets all the credit and the money, while she gets Dick. She is very funny the way she says it. I realized in that moment I mistook her bigboned sweetfaced heavily accented Midwesterness for stupidity. Au contraire. Wonderbread is really funny and smart. She pours another drink, tosses it back hard, and goes off on a mad rant about her painintheassbastard boyfriend who was supposed to propose to her but couldn't pull the trigger. Pull the trigger. She says it again while shooting herself in the head with her fingers. I laugh hard. Feels good. She drinks more. She gives me alcohol. I pretend to drink it. But I don't. It smells like poison. But the more she drinks the more fun she keeps getting.

This is both Real and Easy Money. She has the surf-and-turf special. She's nice and she's a little nervous at first only to get to the intercourse portion of the program. But when she finally gets her feet firmly under her she is a wildcat and a firecracker. I'm working on the whole woman's pleasure garden-of-earthly-delight thing, and Wonderbread seriously digs it.

I do have a flash of slime as I wash up afterwards and get caught in the mirror staring at the miserable plucked chicken who stares back at me. But I have a whole system now. I feel the warm cookie of my money, focus on 3D, and all the treats waiting for me after my trick. This gets me up, out, and over to Sunny's, where I eat ribs slaw and jalapeno cornbread, and suck on beer booze and bong. In 3D you can be liked, admired, and respected even if you are a houseboy. We have our own chicken language, customs, and jokes, just like lawyers, freemasons, and astronauts, and I love being part of that. I dip the cornbread into the barbecue sauce and it lights up the inside of my mouth. I'm hungry all the time these days. Lots of dayold birthday cake and tubs of ice cream. But tonight, in 3D, mercifully, I manage somehow to get full.

When Sunny touches me on the shoulder like family, he makes me feel like I'm King Shit living the High Life.

"Boy, Ah gotta big time opportunity for your ass. An' Ah do mean your ass. Friday night, big ol' costume party, an' you is coe-jully invited. Welcome to the Show, bay-bay!" Sunny does a whoopholler and a funny little dance.

"What do you mean?" I'm equal dollops excitement and terror.

"It's a costume bawl, an' there's gonna be boocoo bucks there, boy. Mo' money, mo' money, mo' money . . ." Sunny's a hog in heaven, lowering his voice as he moves in for the kill. "An' mamma needs a new pair of shoes."

This is why Sunny is Master Pimp. He ties all his charismatic ecstatic love into my ability to make him money.

13

ZEUS

&

DOT

Age is a question of mind over matter.
If you don't mind, it don't matter. — Leroy "Satchel" Paige

X X X

"IT'S A fantastic job, this Friday night, TWO HUNDRED dollars!" Mr. Hartley's straight-shooter baritone reaches down my throat all the way to my seventeen-year-old balls and squeezes hard.

"Wow," I say in what I hope is a loverstudguy voice, but which I suspect smacks of eunuch, "that's great, excellent, thanks, I uh—"

"David," Mr. Hartley sounds like a benevolent dictator in a three-piece suit, the ultimate Master Alpha, "this is a very important client. And if you do this job well I can absolutely guarantee there will be lots of exciting opportunities on the horizon for you. You understand me David? Do we understand each other?"

I have no idea what he's talking about so I say:

"Sure, absolutely, I got—"

"This is a very unique opportunity for you David. I want you to be completely prepared. It's a rather unusual job. But I think it really matches your skill set."

My brain races like a train on bad speed. Will there be barnyard animals involved? Ritual sacrifice? Death masks and scat sandwiches? What will you do for money? Where do you draw your line? How much of your self are you willing to sell for $200?

"David, this client has decided that she wants to treat her friend to a very special birthday gift. You! So get ready to put on your birthday suit." Mr. Hartley laughs like a machine gun rat-a-tat-tat. I laugh too late then stop too quick. "I kid of course," Mr. Hartley plows right on through, "seriously though, David, it's our policy at the Hollywood Employment Agency to give our clients all the information they need to succeed. We believe that preparation is essential to success. So I want you to understand that you are being given by one of our most important clients to her best friend, as a present for her eighty-second birthday."

GULP!

"It's very important to us that our clients are comfortable performing. Are you comfortable, under the circumstances, uh . . . performing . . . David?"

No. No. No. I don't honestly think I can fuck an eighty-two-year-old. That's what I say in my seventeen-year-old manchild idiot head. Out loud I say:

"Sure, absolutely, I'm all over it."

"You're all over it," Mr. Hartley's Uzi of a laugh rattles my skull. "That is droll David, very droll. That's exactly why I thought of you when this job came in. I have every confidence that you won't let me . . . down." Bam Bam Bam Mr. Hartley laughs fast and staccato. "I kid of course. David I want you to call me as soon as this job is done. Do you understand? Do we understand each other?"

"Absolutely, for sure, yeah."

Mr. Hartley gives me the 411. I disconnect.

Immediately my shattered brain sees an ancient naked wrinkled saggy droopy granny spread-eagled in front of me, and my poor placid flaccid penis is a lifeless piece of useless meat, I have to give the money back and I see myself spiraling down humiliated, a brutal failure rejected by Mr. Hartley and Sunny, drummed out of the business, shunned by all my chicken peers, the only family I know at this point who accepts me for what I am, my paycheck my refuge my people, all gone.

✗ ✗ ✗

IF YOU'RE fifteen, and your dad hires me and your best friend to work the graveyard shift at his explosives plant, all alone, on a Saturday night, what would you do?

Graveyard shift. Alone. Saturday night.

To us that can mean only one thing.

PARRRRRRRRRRRRRRRR-TY!

My Dad, a brave industrious immigrant, is now part owner/manager of his very own explosives company: Zeus Powder Company. It sits in the middle of a huge cow field between Dallas and Fort Worth, just outside a little shit-kicking map dot called Euless, Texas. Useless, we call it.

At sunset me and my cousin Mark, a big strapping handsome dude who's my Tonto/Cato/Sancho Panza, we arrive at Zeus in Useless and toil like possessed men-children, shrink-wrapping explosives in maxi-mondo-overdrive. I like to think that Zeus himself had a hand in the miraculous mountain of explosives we shrink-wrap and box. Miraculously, when 1 AM comes strolling down the block, we hit our quota and we're done. Triumphant, we raise our arms and praise the gods, and scream into the parking lot of Zeus Powder Company.

Our lungs sting when we suck in the fire of the Lone Star State night as an infinity of stars twinkle in the big big sky. The first headlights of our fabulous furry freak brothers and sisters appear, and with great glee we greet our sweet revelers, ready to make merry till the longhorns come home, smackdab in the middle of a cow field in Useless, Texas.

Cindy Lou Who, my almost girlfriend, is an up-for-anything Olive Oyl type, all eager knees and elbows, built for speed, if not entirely for comfort. When she steps out of Billy Bob Bobby Joe Willy Dick's hotrod Lincoln in her halter top and microminiskirt, my knees tremor, my heart soars and my cock crows. She leans in to kiss me and the heavy, velvety Jack Danielsy smell seems like the very essence of sex. Tonight's the night. She wants to do It. She told me so. Pleasure center is activated and I am cocked, locked, and loaded, ready to roll.

X   X   X

ANONYMOUSLY KNOCKING on the door in the ultra-fancy swank swish hotel that smells like Olde Money, my mind savagely ravages itself with vicious visions of wrinkled, ravaged, sagging grandmother flesh that shrink-wraps my rapidly shriveling penis. Breath short. Tight. Racehorsing heart pounds against my breastplate. A sticky clammy sweaty nervy jumpy freaky tweaky moisture oozes out of my pores.

I see Kristy shaking her head at me, eyes overflowing with disgust. Who am I kidding, this is who I am.

The door slowly opens. She's trim and pretty in pink rocking a styly Chanel-type suit. She definitely has one of those helmet hairdos, but it's well done. If you like that kind of thing. A huge honking diamond ring holds court on a well tended finger of her left hand. Shoes the same color pink as her outfit. She's got wrinkles but they're not gruesome. She's wearing makeup but it's definitely not Whatever-Happened-to-Baby-Jane-ish. But the best thing about her is the smile. She has a smile that welcomes you in. After a huge sigh full of deep relief the first thought that pops into my seventeen-year-old manchild head is: Shit man, I hope I'm doing this good when I'm eighty-two years old.

Like a hostess greeting an international dignitary, she asks me if I'd like some champagne. Chocolate covered strawberries? Pâté and cheese? It's all spread out on this fancy silvery tray. Curtains are closed. Lights are low. Candlelight makes everything soft. She gives me a long thin beautiful flute of champagne, with a sweet smile ripe with kindness. Like I'm all growed up. It's cool holding a flute.

I know what to do. I've been trained well by my English people.

"I want to wish you a very, very happy birthday."

She holds out her champagne. We clink flutes. We drink. The champagne shoots little giddy meteors tickling my lips and teasing my nose. I love how inside my mouth the most sophisticated Pop Rocks are rocketing. Smooth smooth, smooth, it goes down tingly and frothy, liquid laughter.

She tells me her name is Dorothy. But her friends called her Dot. I think that's a cool name. Dot. She's talking about the champagne. This is from some famous champagne place in France. Soon as I'm done with the first sip I can't wait for another, so I just let it guzzle down my muzzle all twinkly and sparkly. One more big gulp and the whole beautiful flute is empty, the contents now inside me. It comes on quick and suddenly my head is floating on my neck and my face is full of happy bones, my blood rushing like a carefree debutante jitterbugging at her coming-out ball. Life is much greater than it was five minutes ago.

Dot insists I have a chocolate-covered strawberry. Doesn't take much arm-twisting. Apparently it's some world-famous chocolate from Belgium. It's got a hard crunch when you bite it, but then it gets all melty in your mouth as the fruity juice of the rapturously ripe strawberry sings with the chocolate in mind-boggling two-part harmony. When I finish I see Dot watching me with a big grin on her face. Makes me like her. Even more.

Dot tells me she likes to watch people enjoy themselves. I tell her how much I'm enjoying myself. And the crazy thing is I completely mean it. She asks me if I want another one. I say no, even though I really actually do want another one. She asks me if I really want another one but I'm just saying no to be polite. Like she can see right inside my head. I confess I do and did. She insists with an impy grin that I have another chocolate-covered strawberry. So I do. I have two more after that. I could eat every single one. But I am there to do a job. I figure after three chocolate-covered strawberries, it might impair my ability to perform.

Dot tells me all about her madcap romantic husband, how they met, how he proposed to her. Took her to Europe, South America, Broadway shows. She hauls out a picture of him. It's black-and-white. He's in a sharp suit with two-tone shoes, hair all slick and debonair with a devilmaycare smile. I must admit, he was one dapper motherfucker.

He's been dead for ten years. It's sad and happy at the same time. Happy she had him and sad that he's gone. Makes me like her so much that she has all this love for this guy she was married to for like fifty years or whatever. Being the son of a dyke from a home broken beyond repair and having sex for money with grandmothers, I just can't fathom being married to somebody for fifty years. But Dot says her old man was a pistol and a mensch and a big old bundle of fun. Dot tells me about how they used to have these wild and crazy parties with all their fabulous zany friends, where they'd get all dressed up, drinking, dancing and yakking all night about art and politics and life and death and war and taxes.

It's a mad blast listening to her wax about her once wild and precious life. Makes me hope that at some point I can have one. A life. A most excellent wife, some brilliant, crazy, zany friends, a house with a pool and lots of rooms where people can party. Sounds nice.

This is such a great job so far. But of course there's that nagging tug in the back and the pit of my head and belly: how in the name of Pan the horny Goat-Boy am I going to get It up and off? I'm bombarded by the image of my meat torpedo morphing into wet spaghetti. I have to focus extra hard to avoid hyperventilation.

Dot stops talking. She hems and haws and tuts. Clearly she wants to tell me what's on the menu for her birthday dinner, but she's having a terrible time spitting it out.

I'm scared breathless. I desperately want to give Dot want she wants. I need to please her. She's been so nice to me. And I want to succeed at this job. Be an American. Be a man. But will I be able to achieve liftoff with a naked octogenarian laying on top of me? I believe I can. I know I can't. What if she wants to do some weird old-person sex thing I don't know about?

My testes cower in a corner. My head is like a balloon being inflated by a homicidal clown with ADHD. My guts rumble thunderously, roiling like a boiler about to blow.

Again I find myself seriously questioning my career choice.

X X X

JOHNNY BALLS breaks out some world-class Lebanese hash, and excitement sweeps through Useless. There is a rub. Balls forgot to bring matches. Total stoner move.

And so is begun a quest for fire. To our universal astonishment, after an exhaustive search, there is not a match or lighter to be found. We put our collective, albeit feeble, brains together and storm with them, like party-hardy cavemen trying to discover the secret of the sacred flame.

"Cigarette lighter!" someone exclaims.

So we dash, hash-packed pipe bowls in hand, to Billy Bob Bobby Joe Willy Dick's hotrod Lincoln. But no matter how hard we try, the car's cigarette lighter just won't ignite the Lebanese.

Blinded by a flash of inspiration from Pan the Goat-Boy, I remember that the liquid component of Zeus explosives is highly flammable. We could douse paper and cardboard with it, ignite the whole thing with the cigarette lighter from BBBJWD's hotrod Lincoln, and consume the Lebanese. I grab Cindy Lou Who and we blast back into the plant. I snag a plastic bottle full of the maroon colored liquid explosive, grab a bunch of cardboard boxes and paper, and bust out into the parking lot like an addle-brained Athena ejaculating from the forehead of Zeus.

Big Bubba, Little Bubba, Charline-Lynn, Lurline, Elmer, Scorpion, Todd the Toad, Duane the Pain, the bovine Bodine twins, Johnny Balls, Cindy Lou Who, and of course the Man himself, raw-boned, devil-eyed, sharp as the crack of a whip, Billy Bob Bobby Joe Willy Dick, the whole furry freak crew gathers around. We shred the paper products into a pile, and improvise handmade wicks. When I unscrew its top, the crimson colored liquid explosive emits a severe chemical stench that assaults the senses and I can smell my nose hairs singeing. Everyone's breathless, as I pour explosive crimson liquid over shredded paper, and douse several handmade wicks, in the shadow of an explosives factory packed with explosives.

Looking back it seems inconceivable that none of us even stopped for an instant to consider the potential for catastrophic bloodshed, dismemberment, and the splattering of brains all over Useless if a spark somehow ignited the bottle of liquid explosives. It would've blown sky high, which would've triggered a blast inside the plant, and Zeus, along with half of Central Texas, could've been blown to bits in a fiery conflagration of biblical proportions, exploding us all to Kingdom Come.

"15 KIDS KILLED IN EXPLOSIVE PLANT HASHISH TRAGEDY!!!"

But youth is blissfully ignorant, and we gather, poised, with our bowls full of world-class Lebanese hash all ready to smoke, completely unaware that Death is standing there sucking on a bottle of tequila with a worm in the bottom, laughing his ass off at us, just waiting to haul our souls away to Hades.

In the still of the night, with all those teenage hormones bombing up into the vast starry starry Lone Star sky, Billy Bob Bobby Joe Willie Dick yanks the fiery cherry of the cigarette lighter out of the dashboard, and dashes towards us.

Holding breath he sticks his long, liquid-explosive-saturated homemade wick onto the red coils inside the lighter.

Flame blazes as if from the mouth of an angry dragon. He drops his wick onto the shredded liquid-explosive-saturated paper/cardboard. A blast of heat and light mushrooms up into the night, blasting us volcanically backwards with a phantasmagorical force of nature, worthy of Zeus and his lightning bolts.

✗ ✗ ✗

LIKE A tongue-tied eighty-two-year-old schoolgirl Dot forces out this strangulated sentence.

"I've always wanted someone to kiss me . . ." she motions with her head down towards her nether regions, "down there."

That's it? A little head? A wee dram of cunnilingus? That's all she wants? Hell, I can do that with my eyes closed. In fact many times I have. And then I think, Can you imagine wanting to have someone go down on you for fifty years? Having a husband you love and not being able to ask him to kiss you down there? I went down on my girlfriend the first time we had sex. That's how I closed the deal. I've gone down on every girlfriend I've ever had. It seems like one of the most basic sexual things you can do. My mind is officially boggled.

But the weight of the world, weighing so heavy on my head moments ago, has been mercifully lifted. I assure Dot that I would be more than happy to make her dream come true.

She gets under the covers. She doesn't take her clothes off. This is just getting better and better.

Here are the best jobs in order.

1) Just talking.

2) Just talking while I'm naked.

3) Just talking while I'm naked and playing with myself. And by playing with myself of course I mean masturbating.

4) Cunnilingussing.

5) Doggy styling.

6) Missionary positioning.

7) Cowgirling with direct eye contact.

So this is the fourth best job there is.

Dot wiggles and wriggles under the covers. I assume she's taking her old lady foundation garments and underpants off. She doesn't tell me to take my clothes off. So I don't. I crawl under the covers. I suspect there will be lots of wrinkly grandmother flesh. But what do I care? Cunnilingus is cunnilingus. Luckily I was trained in this art by the first girlfriend I ever had, who was much older than me and rigorously demanding, albeit in a very sweet educational way.

It takes a while for me to burrow myself in, but eventually there I am. Right between Dot's 82-year-old legs. It's very dark in there. Like a cave. I like that. And when I arrive, to my surprise it smells good. Fresh. Manicured. Everything is quite smooth leading up to the area. Which is a very pleasant surprise.

Dot is very ironing board tight. But cunnilingusly I've been around the block many times. I take my time. I go slow. I kiss all around her area soft and gentle. Some lips. A little tongue. Very light. The more I do it the more she softens. Then suddenly she's moving herself towards my mouth. Now there are little moans and sighs and groans and gasps coming from outside the covers. How cool is this? I'm thinking, she's totally into it.

I'm so happy to be useful. Usually I'm so useless.

Her hands are on my head now and she's pulling it into her area. And to tell you the truth, her area is much like any other area I've been in. Especially in the depth of this black cave.

Dot is now gently manipulating my head so she's delivering it exactly where she wants it and I'm just applying the appropriate pressure. It's like we're dancing and she's leading while I follow. And she's exhibiting all the symptoms of excitation. It's all happening right there on the tip of my tongue, and I could not be more thrilled.

X X X

SLOWLY THE dust settles, and after it becomes clear that no one has burst into flames, we all coo about how cool it was, and watch with wonderment as the blaze dies down nicely, and the shredded cardboard burns beautifully. We stick unsaturated homemade wicks into the fire and get several bowls going.

The world-class Lebanese hash is even better than advertised. Smooth, cocky, insouciant, an amusing blonde with the kick of a turbo-charged atomic submarine. Certainly worth getting blown up for.

Through my hazy-days confusion I realize I have somehow lost track of Cindy Lou Who. Frantically I turn the plant upside down. Frantic rapidly turns into desperate as Led Zeppelin banshee screams blast out the loudspeakers, booming through Zeus, and I storm around a corner in pursuit of a whole lotta love.

I turn a corner and an embryonic lump is lying on the concrete floor in front of me. You hate to see one of your comrades fallen so early and so hard. As I close in on the lifeless form a horror chills me. It's Cindy Lou Who! I bend down, heart pounding. I move her hair away from her face but to my extreme disgustipation, it's matted thick with puke. I set her head back down gently. She seems okay but I wince as I imagine the nasty hangover waiting in her mailbox. Evidently Lou Who had corn for dinner, because kernels are sprinkled liberally throughout her urp. I wipe the sick off my hand as best I can on her pants. Then I moan out loud as reality kicks me in the groin.

There will be no sex for David tonight. My teeth grit and my fists clench, and I am sure that in my sixteen years on the planet, this is the worst thing that has ever happened to me.

Cousin Mark screeches around the corner crazy-eyed. "Hey man, there's some crazy shit coming down." "What's up?" I bark, sufficiently traumatized. "Somebody squealed," he shrieks.

4:35AM Sunday morning lurches through the door and if you listen closely you can hear the sound of dawn careening around the corner. My stomach flips and a sick settles in its pit as my dad jumps out of his car like his underpants are on fire and strides towards me with furious anger radiating through his grill, preceded by a large vein pulsating mid-forehead.

My next clear memory is sitting in our living room as the sun comes up with my father screaming about what an immature, irresponsible, immoral, selfish, ungrateful, unappreciative, stupid, spiteful, hateful monstrosity I am, while my mom weeps and weeps and weeps. After a while my mind tunes Dad out, his words turn into the barkings of a mad dog of an Englishman. But the more my mom weeps those huge wet mother's tears, the more I can't stop thinking: I am a very very BAD person. I ask for her forgiveness. Then I beg for it.

But no matter what I say, my dad keeps yelling, and my mother keeps crying.

I never again see Useless, nor set foot inside Zeus. Very soon thereafter I am shipped off to boarding school, and Cousin Mark is in the Army. I go into the sex business while attending college. My best friend becomes a nurse in emergency rooms and a raging alcoholic. I become a sitcom actor, coke addict, then a sex addict. Which is not nearly as much fun as it sounds. Cousin Mark is currently doing a long stretch of hard time in prison.

X X X

DOT NOW seems to be climbing the ladder of the stairway to Heaven. I don't know how long we've been going at this, but it doesn't seem that long. And she's already manifesting all the physical manifestations of pre-orgasm. Sure enough, here it comes. Here she comes.

Here comes Dot, diving off the cliff into the sea of sexual ecstasy.

I am overcome with joyful satisfaction. Sunny and Mr. Hartley will be so proud of me.

It's clear we are, you know, done. So I burrow out from undercover and head into the bathroom, to give her a chance to put herself back together. As I eyeball myself in the mirror, I shake my seventeen year-old manchild idiot head. Can you imagine? Eighty-two-year-old grandmother pussy tasted great.

Sure enough, when I come back out, she's totally re-assembled, like nothing happened. The only thing that gives her away is the bloom in her cheeks and the sweet satisfied smile on her lips.

Dot thanks me profusely. She asks me if I would like to take a chocolate -covered strawberry with me. I confess that I would. I grab a chocolate-covered strawberry and head for the door overflowing with well-being. Even though my parents don't really want to talk to me, even though I have no home and no family except for a bunch of prostitutes and a pimp, even though I have no future and I'm wracked by nightmares and lusting for revenge on the man who attacked and shattered me into tattered pieces, at least I'm good at this.

As I'm leaving with my chocolate covered strawberry Dot surreptitiously slips a crisp green bill into my hand while she plants a very nice kiss on my cheek. When I pull back, she playfully wipes the lipstick off my cheek. It's a tiny little gesture, but it feels so intimate and connected in a world where connection is virtually impossible for me.

I thank her profusely—wish her a happy birthday.

She thanks me right back.

Then I'm gone.

It's a $100 bill. Add that to the $200 that was in the envelope on the fancy food platter. So that's $300 to drink fancy French champagne, eat world famous Belgian chocolate-covered strawberries and make one pretty great grandma's dream come true.

As I leave the ultra swank Beverly Hills Hotel, I find myself thinking: America, what a country!

14

TINKERBELL

&

BABY BULLDOGS

You're nobody til somebody loves you. — Dean Martin

NUTHUGGING ELEPHANTBELLS tight as the traffic will allow, sleeveless white T, red hightops, and black wraparound Ray-Bans. This is the state-of-the-art, goin'-to-the-Orgy ensemble Sunny's chosen for me, and when he finishes primping, preening, and Mother Henning me, he closes his eyes to cleanse his visual palette, then pops them open and gives me the once-over twice. He grins. Big.

"Yeaaaaaaah, bay-bay."

Suddenly it's all good.

As Moby Dick glides gracefully through the gilded gargoyle gates of the gaudy Mulholland mansion, limos lounge languidly, Alfa-Romeos pose pompously, and Jaguars graze gluttonously on the punch-drunk pavement.

Butterflies flutter by in my belly. I feel like Cinderella with my glass sneakers, Moby Dick pumpkin, and pimp Fairy Godmother.

✗ ✗ ✗

OUR ALL-AMERICAN rocketship crashlands again, when I'm ten, in Virginia, Minnesota, where one-hundred-and-seven-year-old Scandihoovian men in the forty-seven-below dead of winter jump nude through a hole they cut in the ice, plunge into freezing cold lake water, then sprint back to the one-hundred-and-seven-degree sauna. When you go outside your breath forms little icicles on your eyebrows, eyelashes, and 'stache if you have one. Ten thousand lakes, complete with one billion summer skeeters big as World War II bombers that suck your blood like black bug vampires.

My dad's explosives corporation has sent him just south of the Canadian border so he can stripmine the virgin earth, lopping off trees, blowing holes in our Great Mother, and scooping out her guts.

One winter the snow's so high we climb up on the roof and jump off, flying through the sky, landing in a snowcloud, and sinking slow, swallowed by all that soft cold whiteness, like diving into an ice cream cone.

X X X

MARBLE PHALLI, white and magnificent, support the giant mansion, while roses sleep peacefully in beds. The door's twenty feet high, with a giant lionheaded doorknocker that looks like it would love to take a bite out of your hand.

Sunny gives me the wink and the smile.

I can do this. Woman's pleasure. Loverstudguy.

When Sunny gives the lionheaded knocker a knock, a seven-foot-doorman dressed as a dormouse opens the door as regally as a giant dressed like a rodent can.

Huge music pulsates through the booming woofer-happy sound system. Overhead, a chandelier twinkles like a drag queen on Halloween. Underfoot, the marble floor lies cold, majestic, and butch.

Sunny's a puffed-up rutting peacock who tows me like a houseboatboy into the mansion.

"Hooooooo-ie, Sunny is in de house!"

Voices retort by the score:

"Sunny!!!"

"Look what the cat dragged in!"

"And the cat has got a chicken!"

Sunny's got a line for everyone. A slick wink, a knowing nod, a sticky innuendo. Hundreds of eyeballs train their periscopes on me, and I'm awash in the warm wet heat.

It's one of those times in your life when you know things are either gonna get a lot better or a lot worse.

Marlene Dietrich cruises by with Attila the Hun. Dr. Strangelove's pushed in his wheelchair by Mae West. A six-foot-two Amazon Snow White in a leopard bikini is surrounded by three dwarves dressed as Doc, Grumpy, and the sleaziest Sneezy I've ever seen. A behemoth clad in black leather Death mask, studded collar with leash attached, and rhinestone codpiece walks by on all fours, ridden by a tiny Japanese Madame Butterfly–Lady Godiva woman in heavy Kabuki make-up, lashing him lovingly with her cat-o'-nine-tails.

I feel right at home.

X X X

MINNESOTA SNOW is roof high when I'm eleven. My father's gone, blowing up a mountain, so once again I'm starring in the role of Dad.

The basement's cold, thick, dark, and hard as my mother and I try to midwife our bulldog Gwenyvere, who bulges heavy with puppies, belly distended to monstrous proportions, panting on old blankets covering the floor.

My mom strokes Gwenyvere's head, talking soft and sweet to her while I pet her rump, wet helpless bulldog confusion swelling in Gwenyvere's blood-red eyes. She's begging me to help her. I want to help her. I just don't know how.

Then Gwenyvere goes into hard labor, straining painfully panting and pushing, thick muscles taut tight.

The pups will not come.

The pups will not come.

The pups will not come.

✖ ✖ ✖

OLDE BASTARDS: puffy, grey, and rich.

Middle Men: Fagins making quick slick bucks.

Freaks, Chickens, and Chickadees: leering leather and fresh flesh, bruised body builders and ripped up cheerleaders, cool schoolgirls and hot haunted jocks.

There are three populations at the Ball.

The Olde Bastards clearly have a personal relationship with Death, who sits in their livingroom waiting. We're their Fountain of Youth, and they want to drain us dry.

I watch myself watching them watching us, wrapped in the cocoon of my scar tissue.

Sunny leads me into the reddest room I've ever seen, where a long wooden table leans against the wall like a Noah's Ark of liquor, and two bartenders wearing nothing but hockey masks, cock rings, and black leather gloves wordlessly serve.

A cornucopia of mind-bending brain-numbers are laid out attractively in antique crystal mint dishes: buttons of peyote, magic mushrooms and mda/x, Maui Zaui Hurricane Swirl, Afghani Moses Bull Rush, and Moroccan Fez Blower.

Sunny gives me a silver spoon full of mda/x, and a jolt explodes in my head, as if someone has gently inserted a lit firecracker into my cranium.

Then a warm tingly itsy bitsy spider creeps up my water spout. I want to soak in a giant vat of spumoni, and swim in the river, and feel the waterfall spray in my face.

x x x

COLD HARD dark fills the basement, and into the long thick night my mother and I try to pull puppies out of poor dear Gwenyvere, as she shudders shoving moaning groaning growling howling desperate to deliver.

But the pups will not come.

My mom frantically leaves the vet emergency messages, while Gwenyvere collapses whimpering, head bowed, breath gone.

I lay down with her, nose to smashed-in nose, and when she looks into my eyes I see resignation has moved in. Gwenyvere's eyes shut now with a huge heaving sigh, like her heart-lung machine was just unplugged.

For the first time, I think she will die.

x x x

PETER PAN wears green stiletto humpme pumps, green silk stockings and garter, green satin operalength gloves, plunging green velvet strapless gown, slit to the hilt, and she's packed in puffy tight, flesh hanging out here there and everywhere.

In one hand she grips a whip with a phallic handle, in the other a leash attached to a small young woman in a white wig wearing nothing but a sparkling light on her head.

Tinkerbell.

Sunny jumps in, all Southern smooth, and dishes out the introductions.

"This here is Peter Pan, and . . . Tinkerbell . . ."

"Hello." She's stiff as flint.

"Hi," Tinkerbell smiles shy with high beam eyes. "I'm from Never Never Land."

"Hi," I say, "I'll never grow up."

Tinkerbell is so naked.

Ms. Pan whispers into Sunny and he leans back laughing.

"Boy, why dohncha dance with Tinkerbell?" Sunny gives me the nod, clearly indicating that dance is a euphemism for have wild sex.

With the mda/x, the buzz from the desperate wanting of the Olde Bastards, the adrenaline racehorsing through me, and the soundtrack pounding, I'm mad to go Tinkerbelling.

Peter Pan unhooks her leash, and the girl wearing nothing but the light over her white wig sways with the music. She's small all over. Little girl hands and feet. Little freckles. And, like all my poultry peers, sometimes she looks twelve, sometimes she looks forty.

Then she locks into me with big crooning baby blues, and we're rhythmically in synch, in utero, bump for bump, grind for grind, tribal shaking, lust loose in a loin lock, lost in each other's music.

Tinkerbell digs herself into my shoulders. I yowl and thump her into me so our chests hit hard. My teeth rip into her neck with nothing but sheer instinct, and Tinkerbell screams in blood pleasure.

I suck hard on a mouthful of her neck. Pulling my hair hard, she rips my head from her flesh, where a red welt blossoms. I growl and smack a loud slap on her ass. Tinkerbell's on fire with desire, high and higher, and lashes her tongue out yelping, piercing her nails into my back. I shout cuz it feels good while it hurts, heavy lovesweat flying off us as the crowd oozes and ahs, and all that juice fills me and thrills me: Damn, this is the most fun I have ever had in my life!

I have a vision. I see me and Tink in the Smokey Mountains, a little log cabin with some cows and pigs and chickens, deep in the woods, growing cornonthecob, making little freak babies.

I can see it so clearly.

X X X

THICK HARD dark cold black night envelopes a huge white baby bulldog head that appears from between Gwenyvere's hind legs. Eyes closed, it hangs half in the world and half in the womb. Then shoulders ribs hindquarters and feet plop out with great gobs of goo, and a perfect baby dog slides onto the blanket on the basement floor in a puddle of blood and guts and Godknowswhat.

Lord, it's a big ol' pup. Enormous. Doesn't seem anatomically possible that this huge thing could come out of her, even though I just watched it happen.

Gwenyvere, the proud new mother, is relieved beyond belief, and pops out two much smaller pups, half as big, easy as you please, then happily starts slurping off the thin clear sausage shrinkwrap covering them up.

My mom and I dance like punchdrunk midwives as the pups squirm when she laps them with that huge wet tongue. Watching those new pups vibrating with life, there's no way around it: This is a miracle.

X X X

STROBE LIGHTS turn everything into stop-action kinetic Picasso orgy snapshots. Slender arms pendulum breasts thigh cheese lip meat calves dangling bloodbank eyes and shaved coochies stick together in impossible angles.

Tinkerbell's giving me more pleasure than seems humanly possible, vaporlocked on me, dancing the mouth mambo.

Osweetbabyjesusmothermary&joseph.

I look down at Tinkerbell, who looks up at me at the exact same instant, like we've rehearsed the move many times, and we beam dreamy creamy smiles at each other. I could rescue her from this Peter Pan asshole. We could start our own chicken business, Marx style, from each according to ability, to each according to need. We could make a shitload of money, then go live on an island somewhere. Make beautiful babies that get brown in the sun. I wish I knew her name.

The crowd crowds round, leaning in so they won't miss a trick, the heat of the spotlight even hotter as Peter Pan flicks Tinkerbell with her whip and Tink wraps herself around me. The crowd sucks a gasp. I close my eyes and the rapture flows through Tinkerbell and into me in an endless, sensuous Mobius strip.

With careful orchestration, split-second timing, and shrewd momentum management, Sunny has turned me, the simple son of Immigrants, into the catalyst for a take-no-prisoners, lifestyles-of-the-rich-and-famous, oldfashioned newfangled orgy.

That's why I love America.

X X X

EYES SHUT tiny tight, the puppies wiggle and wriggle and squiggle on the blanket, getting the life licked into them by Gwenyvere, who's mama bulldog proud.

My mother and I shake hands, shake our heads, and make many happy sounds while those teeny tiny puppies twist and fidget, trying to figure out what the hell's going on in this big old world.

Then I notice the first, too-huge baby. It's not moving. Gwenyvere won't touch the still giant. She pushes the other two away from it hard with her smushed-in face, then licks them like baby bulldog Popsicles.

My mom looks at me. Gwenyvere seems too busy loving the alive pups to care that her firstborn is lying lifeless in afterbirth. My mother puts the huge not-moving one next to Gwenyvere, but she shoves it with her muzzle all the way off the blanket onto the cold hard basement floor. Then she goes back to mothering her other pups.

Oh, my. That big baby bulldog is dead.

x x x

TINKERBELL SHOWERS me with snowflake kisses, a mad hunger flowing between us as we ride around on each other in the middle of this love zoo at the height of mating season.

Yeah, an island somewhere in the South Pacific. We'll rent a hut on the beach for fifty cents a day. Catch fish, eat mangoes, roll around in the sunset.

Then I hit a spot in Tinkerbell and she pours soaring into me roaring a Jungle scream.

The orgy comes to a full stop and we're once again right in the center of America, all eyes upon us, and Oh, it's good in there, one big writhing amoeba feeding me feeding her.

Peter Pan eyeballs me mean and hard. She grabs Tinkerbell and with a loud popping sound drags her away.

Tink looks back sad at me. She doesn't want to go. I don't want her to go. Then she disappears through the Sea of Freaks back to Never Never Land.

x x x

DEADWEIGHT OF giant pup in hands, thick and dumbfounded in my parka as the hard day is born, it's my job to bury the huge, lifeless baby bulldog.

It's cold as death this morning as I brush snow from the ground and put the stilllife down, his eyes locked shut forever.

I try to dig a grave, but the shovel bounces off the stone ground, and Mother Earth will not open herself and accept this little dead baby.

The deceased white pup's the same color as the snow.

Finally I manage to chisel the shallowest of graves, and into the dark hard hole I put the baby giant. I cover it up with dirt and snow, then look up and try to pray. But I have nothing to say, and it seems like no one is up there.

x x x

HUMP TIME zone is where I've been hanging for I know not how long, in and out of more holes than a hungry gopher. A tattoo of a shark swims across a Botticelli bottom. A Ku Klux Klan Grand Wizard has his white bottom paddled by a man Aunt Jemima. The three-hundred-pound behemoth is forced into positions of humiliation by the ninety-pound Madame Butterfly, who whips him until welts sprout like fleshflowers, then whispers sweet nothings in his ear.

Suddenly I come to, like a caterpillar awakening from a butterfly dream. I look over at Sunny and he nods at me, opening a side door.

Then we're floating home in our Moby Dick pumpkin chariot through the alabaster night, a black crow hanging high in front of a big fat moon.

"Ya done good, boy," Sunny says.

"Thanks, Sunny," comes up out of me.

I finally feel good.

For about ten seconds. Then I want someone to suffer like I do.

15

HOOP RAGE

Anger is a short madness. — Horace

HALFWAY DOWN Immaculate Heart College's hill lives the basketball court. There's not alotta sports action at IHC, it being a nun school and all, but this afternoon there's a nice three-on-three situation working as the sun continues its perpetual Hollywood shine. My fellow hoopsters are out for a little lite hoops, looking to break a mini-sweat, knock down some j's, go hard to the hole, do some minor white-boy balling and smack talking.

Me, I'm having one of those days. Layups roll around the rim before dribbling off miserably. Passes clang off my frying-pan hands. Jumpers thud hard off iron. I'm throwing up enough bricks to build a house with my three-little-piggie friends, and I can just see the Big Bad Wolf hiding behind a tree waiting to eat a grandmother.

I'm swearing loud now. I'm a very good swearer. It's a kind of speaking in tongues, ecstatic religious release for me.

"Cocksuckingpigbastardscumsuckingpissboy!"

Everyone's looking at me funny, like there might be something seriously wrong with me. Whatever. There's nothing in my universe now but this silly little pickup game, and the rage bubbling up in deep wells where I've stored it away for just this kind of occasion.

X X X

I'M THIRTEEN. Our All-American Dream Tour has stopped in Dallas. Mom and Dad's ship has finally landed, thirty miles away in Useless, where my father is part-owner and ruler of Zeus Powder Company.

My mom doesn't see my dad for days at a clip, and when he is around he eats, sleeps, and attacks the yard with power tools at the same furious pace.

But now he's an Executive. The milk and the honey are here at last. The coal miner's son has struck gold.

X X X

BUMPING, GRINDING, and shoving on my guy, I'm digging the hitting, goading him to retaliate. And the madder I get the worser I play. The ball's bouncing off my knee, fumbling through my hands, and sliding through my butterfingers.

I'm D-ing up on my guy now. He tries to drive past me, only I slide over and hipcheck him, flashing one of my Minnesota hockey moves in Tinsel Town. I knock him off balance, and he loses the ball out of bounds.

He calls a foul.

"Foul? Bullshit! That's no foul. You think that's a foul? That's just good D making you look bad, baby!"

My guy looks around sheeplike, seeking support from his teammates, who shuffle around like they're looking for spare change, not wanting to get dragged into my theater of cruelty.

Finally a guy on my team sighs. "Yeah, man, I thought you fouled him."
And this guy's on my team.

"That's a foul? Oh, I'm sorry, I wish someone had told me we were playing pussyball."

I grab the ball and put it right in my guy's face. "Okay," I say, "let's play some pussyball."

My guy looks at me like I'm a genetic engineering project gone horribly wrong.

I can barely focus on the game now, just waiting for the opportunity to pound the shit out of my guy, who's getting rid of the ball too quick, watching me out the corner of his eye, giving me too much room when I have the ball.

I bide my time, crouched low in the tall grass while the angrypsycho talks on the audio track in my brain: you wanna see a foul, I'll show you a foul, ya pieceoshitmotherbastardcumburpingbitch.

Then suddenly my golden moment unfolds in slow motion as my guy turns the corner dribbledriving around the foul line. He's lost track of me, thinks he beat me to the spot, but I'm one step ahead of him, playing hide and seek behind his teammate.

And now he's mine.

As my guy leaves his feet to go up for the layup he's slightly off balance, concentrating on the rim, while I line him up in the crosshairs, coiling, poised, springloaded with stored-up venom.

X X X

MY BODY is all growed up when I'm fifteen. I play soccer with my dad's team in Dallas, and they're a very good team, league champs, mostly expatriate Brits. Playing against a brutish team, a burly stocky defender viciously hacks me. I crumble howling, clutching my Achilles where I've been violated. I get up tough, so all my dad's teammates know what a coldblooded bastard I am, and tell the hard man who hit me to piss off. My old man busts over, and after he makes sure I'm okay, points at my attacker, and marks him with the evil eye.

About ten minutes later the marked man gets the ball, and out of nowhere my old man materializes and eviscerates him like a knight slaying the Jabberwocky. The other team goes mad, and the ref threatens to expel my dad from the game. But he stands tall over my fallen attacker, and tosses me a little wink that no one else can see.

My father has punished mine enemy.

X X X

HIGH ON bile, I fly at my guy, slamming the sharp blade of my shoulder into his sternum, OH MY GOD it feels good, that deep down bodycrunch, me solid mass, him offkilter bantamweight, the visceral inflicting thrill pulsing through my pleasure centers.

His body jackknifes backwards, torso slingshotting away, while his bottom half stays where it is for a moment, then follows the top half, knees and elbows akimbo.

He hits the asphalt with his left elbow and the side of his left knee, scraping layers of skin onto the asphalt, and grinding to a halt with shocked pain spreading across his face.

"Is that a foul? Cuz where I come from, that's what we call a foul!" I roar, towering over him like a false god.

My guy touches the open wound on his knee, and his hand comes back with blood. He touches his elbow. More blood. He looks from the blood to me. Back to the blood. Then back to me.

"What the hell is wrong with you?" The hurt of a child who's been punished for no reason at all.

I could've broken his ribs. We could be scraping his brain off the blacktop. What the hell *is* wrong with me?

Everyone stares at me like I'm unfit for human company. I shrink instinctively and trot out the apologies.

"Sorry, man. I'm so sorry. I guess I'm a little . . ."

A little what? Psycho? Homicidal?

I reach out my hand to help him up. He turns it down.

"You got a problem, man."

Everyone agrees. They help him up.

"Hey, I'm sorry man, that's just the way we play where I come from." Where's that, Sing Sing? "Your ball, man, sorry." I'm trying to pretend everything's normal, but nobody's playing along.

"No, I'm done," my guy mumbles, hobbling away like a war hero after a senseless bombing.

Then I'm alone, the hole in my bucket a little bigger.

16

HERE CUM DE JUDGE

Power tends to corrupt and absolute power corrupts absolutely. — Lord Acton

"WE'RE HAVING a big bash at my parents' house on Easter, and I was wondering if you, uh, wanted to come."

And there it is. The invitation. Kristy wants me to meet her Mommy and Daddy, Suicidal Sis, and Marty the German shepherd.

"Yeah, I'd really like to meet your folks." An actual note of sincerity, as excitement once again kisses terror.

Now all I have to do is get through my date with the Judge. Apparently the Judge saw me at the orgy and asked for me. Sunny told me I wouldn't have to have sex with him. I made my, "Oh yeah, right!" face, but he swore there'd be no sex with the Judge. And it's a $500 job. This stopped me dead. $500.

"No sex? You swear?" I lean into the question.

"Ah swear on my dead pappy's asshole! The Judge, he don't go with no boys, but he likes to git hisseff roughed up a li'l bit. An' he's a big fan of yo's."

Five hundred clams to rough up a judge? Big fan of mine? Sure, why not? Then I'll quit all this chick and chit and move in with Kristy.

x x x

"NIGHT, MOM," I soprano as I toodle off to beddybyes one night in my early adolescence.

During the night my testicles drop like a couple of lodestones in a bowl of pea soup.

"Good morning, Mother. Hope you slept well!" booms out of me in a breakfast baritone the next morning, and suddenly I'm fevered with curiosity, mad as a hatter with a hard-on.

Sex.

What goes in where and how?

x x x

THE JUDGE comes out of the bathroom in a judge's robe. Sunny told me he was a judge, but I didn't expect him to actually wear his judge's robe. I arrived at the Griffith Park apartment about ten minutes ago, found the key under a loose brick, and let myself in as instructed. There was no one there, and I had a mini-mal panic seizure. G-men in closets. SWAT team swooping down and busting my ass. I scanned the room. Elegant and simple. Antique table, two chairs, and a Frenchish desk on which sat a manila envelope. Just like Sunny said. I relaxed. A little. A white envelope was hiding inside. I scooped it out carefully and opened it slowly. Inside were five naked hundred-dollar bills that make me safe and warm. They fit so nice in my pocket. $500 for an hour. I *am* hot.

A typed note, folded in half, crouched in the envelope, containing explicit instructions involving me, the Judge (who referred to himself throughout as "The Judge"), and a metal-edged ruler.

How far I've come in my career, I thought, from telling women how beautiful they are while I'm naked, to telling a Judge how horrible he is while he's naked.

X X X

WHITE GOO oozes from the eyes of the clerk who lurks behind the counter of the Pink Pussycat. One rotten tooth sits like a black plank in the middle of his cankerous cavern of a mouth. His head is too small for his body.

When I ask for change, hovering in the comfort of the Shadow, a deep, wet, eighteen-wheeler of a hack rumbles up the highway of the clerk's lungs, and he hands me four droopy drooling quarters.

"Thank you," I chirp, cheery as a cherry popover. I have recently turned thirteen.

The Pink Pussycat teems with heaps of steaming mags and sweaty video tapes. Hot Pink Wet Virgin Slut Cheerleader Lesbo Nuns. Loads of lone wolves with cigarette breath and damaged skin play pocket pool, ogle the magazines, and fondle the Plastic Love Dolls.

"Marilyn comes complete with silky hair. All organs are realistic in every detail. Heavy duty vacuum bulb builds up amazing suction. Make her as skinny or as buxom as you want. Don't be fooled by cheap breakable imitations. Be the stud you always wanted to be."

X X X

BURNING THE instructions as instructed and putting the ashes in the sink gave me a real Mission: Impossible jolt. If I'm caught or killed the secretary will disavow any knowledge of my actions.

The matches waited by the sink next to the old-fashioned metal-edged ruler. The Judge doesn't miss a trick. Guess that's why he's the Judge. I lit a match and ignited the instructions. Puff of flame, smell of sulphur. I dropped it in the sink like a flaming dead Viking being floated out to sea.

I picked up the ruler with the cold metal edge, and it made a nice loud whack sound when I smacked it into my palm.

A muscle memory hit me, and wham! I was back in George Wallace Elementary School. My third grade teacher, the ninety-seven-year-old Mrs. Bronte, the dreaded Brontosaurus, all three-foot-nine of her, was dragging out the old metal-edged ruler to thrash some poor sucker's knuckles, the sixty-four eight-year-olds in my class smelling blood, silently wild with delight.

✗ ✗ ✗

FLORESCENT PINK signs shine like flaming flamingos in the Pink Pussycat, describing in a child's uneven scrawl the films being shown in each booth.

2 SLUTS WIT A STUD.

2 STUDS AND A SLUT.

A STUD, A SLUT, AND A SHEPLAN PONEE.

I don't want all the bells and whistles. I'm thirteen, horny as a schoolgirl and nervous as a sailor, and I just want to see a normal guy and a normal gal doing what normal people do when they Do It. It never dawns on me that I might be in the wrong place to see anything like that.

✗ ✗ ✗

GRAY ON gray is the Judge, in all his robed glory, skin hanging flaccid cheek-by-jowl, dangling waddle wobbling over his collar, ushering a sour graveyard smell in with him.

As soon as I lay eyes on him I feel mean and hateful. I can see the Olde Bastard looking down from the bench with righteous condescension, telling me what a menace to society I am.

I slap the ruler hard into my hand, a loud smack, and it hurts, which helps, like Bruce Lee tasting his own blood. The Judge jumps, and that feels good.

"You're a miserable piece of shit, aren't you?" I stride right over to him all revved up Clockwork Orange-style and I punch him knuckle on nose.

That's what I want to do. What I really do is stop my fist inches from the Judge's face, which registers high-voltage fright as he quivers in rapture and terror.

"Yes," he whimpers, "I need—"

"Shut up, bitch!"

I push him back into the wall, and he slumps with a thump. I tear the robe off him and shove him down. Guess what the Judge has on under his robes.

Diapers.

I find myself seriously questioning the American judicial system.

X X X

ONE STUD, one slut, sooper hot hot hot

I'm pretty sure that's as normal as it's gonna get at the Pink Pussycat. Inside the booth it smells like an old moldy sperm sandwich. I slip a quivering quarter into the slick slot, and when a small screen flickers to life, a woman's face appears. She's cockeyed. One eye goes east, one goes west, one flies over the cukoo's nest. Her make-up is buckwheat-pancake thick. A soundtrack of bad wackawacka guitar and synthesized drum-machine wheezes under the sludgebucket basso profundo moan of a man loaded on testosterone.

"Oh baby. Give it to me you nasty little baby. You love it, don't you baby? Oh baby, baby, baby."

She moans but no sound comes out. Then I hear a moan when her mouth isn't moving. It's out of kilter. Out of sync. Cockeyed.

She glances off-camera, and you can almost hear some dictator director shouting:

"Act sexy!!!"

One eye darts back to the camera, while the other drifts off somewhere as she licks her lips and rolls her eyes. She's not sooper hot at all. She's sad in one eye and gone in the other.

✗ ✗ ✗

DISHING OUT brutal abusive humiliation is usually not an option with your boss, no matter how horrid he may be. But that's what I'm getting paid for. I let loose a nice long sadistic laugh as I look at this sad olde gray bastard on his knees, with his flabby saggy man tits, big pregnant cannon-ball gut, puddly thighs, and hunched shoulders grown wild with a nasty forest of white hairs.

In his diapers.

"Hey," the Judge starts indignantly, "wait a—"

"Did I tell you to talk? No. You talk when I tell you to, you fat little prick—"

"Yes, I am, I'm a fat little prick!" he dribbles.

"Shut the hell up, bitch!" I hiss, pissed, whacking him with the flat part of the ruler across the middle of his back, a howl yowling out of him as he bellyflops on the floor.

"Does your wife know you like to wear diapers? Do all the lawyers and judges know you like to cum in your diapers? Answer me!"

"No," the Judge snivels.

"No, sir, bitch!" I snarl.

"No, sir . . ." the Judge whines.

His fear feeds me, and I gorge ravenously. But it's like stuffing yourself with dayold birthday cake that you know is gonna make you sick later.

"Put your hands out in front of you," I rumble.

This command comes with a smack of the ruler on his fat belly, accompanied by a tremendous slapping sound. The Judge averts his eyes like I'm the Pope, and sticks his gray spotted hands out in front of him. I've got this rich pillar-of-society prick right where I want him.

X X X

A PLASTIC champagne glass is in one of Cockeyed Girl's hands, and in the other a veiny, blood-engorged wangdangdoodlehammer that she glances at sideways, like it might take a bite out of her cheek.

The screen goes dark. I desperately need to know what happens to my distressed porno princess, so I ram in another quarter, and there she is, exactly where I left her, licking her lips again, rolling her eyes back in her head like a tropical fish about to plunge into a coma, and winkling the wangdangdoodlehammer into the plastic champagne glass.

My femme fatale looks offscreen in a panic. "Do I have to?" flashes across her face. Apparently she does, cuz then she looks back at the camera, does her pseudosexy face again, and chugs the whole thing down.

Bottoms up!

X X X

"SHUT YOUR eyes!" I bark to the diapered Judge kneeling with his hands held in front of him. He closes them instantly. I like that. He's breathing hard and sweating like a fat old pig having sick sex.

I silently slide behind him, rear back and smack him hard with the ruler on the pink bottom of his soul, catching his foot flush with another tremendous thwack that tingles deliciously all the way through my central nervous system.

The Judge tumbles like Humpty Dumpty off his wall, whimpermoaning in little rhythmic spasms. I plant my foot in the middle of his back and crush him into the beige carpet, where he quakes with the secret creepy excitement a Judge can only get from being trashed by a boy chicken he's paying five hundred dollars.

I feel sorry for the Judge. Who pumped their poison into this poor guy? One part of me wants to stop and try to make him feel better.

But I can't. This feels too good.

X X X

COCKEYED GIRL cocks one eye into the camera, looking like a sick kid who just swallowed a poisoned-pea pellet. Her other eye wanders away forlorn. The unheard offscreen commandant orders her to smile, and as she snaps back, the east eye smiles sicklysweet, while the west eye looks like it's about to cry.

Sex? That's sex? Shocked and wobbly, I reel and teeter, jellykneed. I stumble into the supercool of the Pink Pussycat black light, lean against the booth to regroup, then stagger through the flaccid limp love beads, roll past the drooling troll behind the counter, and get ejaculated through the front door, where the blast of blinding white light brings reality rushing back like the four o'clock uptown express.

When my life flashes before my eyes this is one of the things I'll see: that beatup cockeyed ghost of a girl flickering away.

X X X

MOANGROANING LOUD now the Judge bucks and thrashes, crying out somewhere between a wheeze and a sob. Watching this fat olde bastard busting his nut in his diapers makes my skin slink away in shame and my brain revolt. How did I end up doing this? That's it for me. I gotta get out.

The Judge finally stops and looks up at me. Seeing his ashen sicksad deathmask face makes my temperature drop thirty degrees, and I shiver

the shiver of the damned. I grab my helmet, check my money, and mutter,
"Later . . ."

Whatever.

17

PSORIASIS, DEEPFREEZING,

&

WHERE ARE MY KEYS?

You always hurt the one you love,
the one you shouldn't hurt at all. — Fisher/Roberts

X X X

EASTER MORNING I wake up with a head full of chainsaws and out-of-tune violins, while my dead brain cells are getting a twenty-one-gun salute. My hovel has never looked so squalid. I have no memory of Saturday night after a tequila-drinking contest with a red bloated ex-sailor who had a tattoo of Popeye on his forearm he could make dance by wiggling his muscles. The drunker we got, the funnier Popeye danced.

Thank God my motorcycle helmet is on the floor near my bed. Thank God my head's not in the helmet, rolling down an off-ramp of the Hollywood Freeway.

I try to get up. Big mistake. Whole new levels of pain bells ring in my head, my chest, and all the way down through my balls to the balls of my feet. The effort overwhelms me, and I land back on the too-thin mattress that barely functions as my bed.

I manage to drag myself into the all-fours position, and pause here for quite some time, although time is particularly relative now, agony extending seconds like a stopwatch's hangover. I'm exhausted and I haven't been awake five minutes.

Easter. Kristy. What time is it? Shit. I look for my miserable little clock, but I can't find it, and it hurts too much to keep looking.

Ever since Mommy and the orgy I've felt compelled to hang at Immaculate Heart College playing frisbee and ping pong with people I don't even like just so I can be with other kids my age who aren't industrial sex technicians. So Easter with Kristy's parents looms ahead like Mecca just past the Valley of Death, hope and longing lurking skittishly with the dread that they'll see me for the whore I am. And I've already created a waking nightmare for myself by sheepdipping my head in cheap liquor last night.

RIIIIIIIIIIIIII-NG!

When the phone goes off it feels like a tiny hand grenade got dropped in my ear hole and exploded inside my skull. A puke wave erupts from my stomach gushing up toward my throat. A heavy groan moans out of me and the Herculean effort of suppressing the sick makes pain shoot through me nose to toes. My first impulse is that it's Kristy, and I'm late. I'm supposed to be at her house at noon, and God knows what time it is. I rush, or try to get somewhere near the speed of rush through the cold oatmeal I seem to be stuck in, still fully dressed in last night's alcohol-drenched nicotine-stenched clothing. Arid and parched, I cross the vast expense of livingroom desert, and throbbingly grab the phone.

"Hooo-ie, how you doin', bay-bay?"

It's Sunny. Of course. Who else would it be?

"I'm good, man, what time is it?" Sour's in my mouth, I need to pee and possibly shit. And shower. Now.

"'leven," Sunny coos.

I breathe easier. Got a little time.

"How you doin'?" manages to mutter out of me.

"Cool as a cucumber up an Eskimo's asshole."

I chuckle. Big mistake, as a cranial ache pulsates nine and a half on the Richter scale, and climbing with a bullet.

"Par-ty, bay-bay! Ah got me a new bonnet with awll the frills upon it, an' Ah'll be the finest fay-ree in the Easter parade!"

I hear the drums beating the call of the wild.

x x x

MOM HURRICANES around the house, fixing her huge bouffanty frosted helmethead, roasting beef, making tetties and Yorkshire puddings, preparing my brother and sister for presentation, straightening the house.

As a four-year-old, I remember thinking how strange that is. To straighten the house. I see our crooked, crippled house, and my mother desperately trying to straighten it.

My mom's all sweetness and light as my dad gets home from work and we sit down for dinner. We say the grace we always say:

"God is great, God is good, and we thank him for our food."

I'm bothered by the fact that good and food don't rhyme.

x x x

"THANKS, MAN, but I got a date." I'm firm in my hungover resolve to choose life.

"Ohhhh, you gotchoo some nice coed pussy—well, ain't that sweet? Bring 'er awn over." Sunny coos.

Kristy, these are my wacky child-prostitute friends. Cruella, say hello to my lady.

"Naw, I don't think so." I'm firm.

"Well hell, cum awn by when you done gittin' pussywhupped, and you can have some of my chocolate aiggs." Sunny almost makes you believe life really is a cabaret.

"In your dreams, baby."

"They'z gonna be some Easter bunnies with some tight li'l baskets for yo' ass," Sunny hisses hypnotically.

Visions of 3D overflowing with freaks and friends and a sweet baby for me dance like sugarplum fairies in the pin of my head.

Now wait a minute, hold on one God damn second here, you are not jumping down that hole. Barbecue, watermelon, cornonthecob, Mom, Dad, Dog, Suicidal Sis, Kristy's Easter Sunday, end of discussion, case closed.

This is your ticket out of all the shit, boy.

"Thanks man, but I, you know, got this thing I gotta do . . ." That's as firm as it gets for me right now.

"Aw-ite, but just in case you change your mind, Ah'll keep a bunny warm for ya. Oh, an' Ah got a real nice job for you Mun-dee night—easy money, boy, five hunnert. An awll you gotta do is act natch-ally."

Sunny as master carrot dangler.

"Thanks man, but n- . . .n- . . .n-"

The word No forms in my brain, and travels all the way to the tip of my lips, but I just can't get it out.

"You hear me, boy?" Sunny's peevey snippiness tweaks my already tweaked brain.

"Yeah, absolutely. My roommate was just talkin' to me—Yeah, I'll take care of that—Uh, sure, job Monday, that's cool, five hundred, yeah . . ." I'm shaky, I can hear I am.

"You aw-ite, boy? Somethin' botherin' you?" Sunny sounds like a fight doctor whose prizefighter has just taken a shot to the head.

"No, I'm cool," I lie. Ever since the Judge I've been snappish, brittled, fraying, ready to bite someone's head off. Not cool at all.

"An' Ah almost forgot, that goil Jade's gonna be here tonight, she told me she like to git together whichew." Sunny knows where every button is, and he's pushing them all.

Jade invades my brain and I feel her in my belly. Jade in a slinky kinky dress, with those sleepy almond eyes dancing to the music in her head.

No. You're going to Kristy's parents, you're going to be the perfect boyfriend, and I don't wanna hear one more word about it.

"Tell her to give me a call."

I'm proud I could say no.

"Aw-ite, well, good luck boy, you gonna need it. An' remember, when you git tired of awll that prissy pussy, you come awn down, and we tighten your wig for ya."

Sunny chuckles. Then he's gone.

X X X

PSORIASIS BREAKS out in red patches of anger on Mom's elbows and scalp. Something's off at the dinner table. Way off. Even as a four-year-old I can see that. My mom's pissed my dad off, and there's an edgy terror to everything. He's not speaking to her. He babbles on about the spotted dick we're having for desert, and how much wind he broke at work, but not a word to my mother.

Not one word. Not a nod nor a wink. Nothing.

My mom wrings her hands and itches her psoriasis.

X X X

MY HUNGOVER head hurts worse when I hang up the phone. Who am I kidding? Kristy's folks will recognize a damaged mind when they see one and give me the bum's rush. I'm going to Sunny's.

No. Stop. Get in the shower, get your shit together, walk out the door, get on the bike, go over to Kristy's parents' house, and nicely be her Easter boy.

But as I shower and dress in my blue buttonup shirt and my green corduroys, I can't get around the fact that getting dolled up and acting

normal for Kristy and her folks sounds like dental surgery. Her parents
are probably uptight prigs. Hey, I don't have to perform like some trained
monkey for Kristy and her dumbass Daddy and Mommy.

Whereas if I go to Sunny's I can just be a whore.

And Jade is gonna be there. Jade asked about me.

There are moments in all of our lives when we're faced with choices
that make us who we will become.

Kristy v. Sunny.

But first, before I choose anything, I must have a nervous breakdown.
And to do this I need something to focus all my fury on.

My keys.

X X X

DAD DEEPFREEZES my mom and doesn't speak to her for three weeks. Just
cuts her off cold. Breakfast, dinner, weekends. Will not speak to her.
The message is clear. This is what a husband does when he's mad at his
wife: deepfreeze her.

The reason my dad wouldn't speak to my mom, I found out recently,
was that she'd had a washing machine accident and flooded the basement,
causing some water damage.

X X X

KEYS KEYS keys. Where are my keys?

"Does Braddy love Mommy?"

Flabby judge wobbles in grotesque rapture.

Tinkerbell floats away forever.

Change the record, Chowderhead.

It's getting so I can't find a happy record with a beat I can dance to. All
my records seem to be soundtracks to my own personal horror movies.

I look in the mirror and a harrowed haunted shattered teenager looks back at me. I'm my own portrait of Dorian Gray, and my sins stare me right in the face.

I can do this. Go to Kristy's. Get myself out of this nasty life. Maybe her Old Man can get me a job. Move in with her, maybe. Yeah, that's a good thought to hold on to.

Now all I have to do is find my keys.

In the pocket of my denim jacket, there are no keys. The old roadkill door I found and transformed into a desk is overflowing with detritus: pens stolen from banks with the chains still attached; little bits of paper filled with scribbles of names, numbers, song lyrics, philosophical treatises, rants and raves; a leftover cake container and a dead pint of ice cream; soiled coins, dark wadded dollars; a pair of glasses with eyeballs attached to slinkies that shake around and wobble when you put them on and move your head.

But no keys. Shit. I always leave my keys here. This is where I leave my keys. Damn. Look at all this pitiful useless shit. This is my life?

Stop. Where was the last place I saw the keys? Actually, I have no memory of my keys. Do I even have keys?

Stop. Keys. A pair of shorts on the floor. Maybe they're in there. Loose change, pack of matches, Tootsie Pop.

No keys. Shit!

In the livingroom I look on the Salvation Army foldable cardtable, and in plastic milkcrates that are doing time as endtables.

No keys.

Into the bathroom. Maybe I swallowed them and they came out when I took a shit.

No keys.

Not in the shower. Not on the floor. Not under the rug.

Into the kitchen. Where are my keys? Keys, keys, keys. Not on the floor. Not in the sink. Under the sink? Who knows, I was stone drunk, it's possible. I bend down, open the cabinets, and poke my head into the dark under there, soaking in the Clorox-ammonia potpourri.

No keys.

I back out.

BAM!

My head hits the sink with a thick thud.

Motherbitchdickfacebastardpussyassshit!!!

The head was just starting to feel normal after being in the Battle of the Bulge all morning, but the hurt bounces around inside now like a pinball of pain—

TILT! TILT! TILT!

A hopping madman I am holding my throbbing skull. I punch the kitchen wall with my fist. I expect to break a hole in it with my fury, but it doesn't give at all, and a whole new pain takes a bite out of my knuckles, cranking up the volume knob in my head. The hurt humps its way up my arm and into my spine before it rattles down into my ass.

"Sonofadogsuckingdickwadbitch!!!"

Totally out of my mind, I smashmouth off the walls down the hall, pissed-off radiating out of me like plutonium.

Where are my God damn keys?

Suddenly I'm back in my hovel, picking up fistfuls of desktop detritus and flinging them against my stained-rug walls as hard as I can, scattering my worthless crap to the four corners of my miserable little universe.

Splat! Splatter! Whack!

Then I pick up my shitty grandad roadkill chair, raise it over my head and smash it down as hard as I can. It hits the floor with a satisfying crack, and explodes, transforming instantly into kindling.

It's unclear how smashing my chair was going to help me find my keys, but at the time it seems like exactly the right thing to do. Plus it feels so good.

I pick up the doortabletop, hold it over my head, and ram it hard into a hanging mirror, and oh man, that bastard shatters into a million jagged sharp shards that rain down like confetti in hell.

The smashed glass makes me take a step back. I take it all in. My little hellhole looks like it threw itself on a landmine to save the rest of the platoon. When I get my breath back I collapse onto my nasty slagheap mattress, a postcoital wrungout calm balming over me.

Hey, maybe I should have a wee little nap.

Then I'm asleep.

I wake up floating in the debris of my life. The thought of even calling Kristy now makes me shrivel like a spider on a hotplate, and in one swift instant I dismiss the thought.

When I realize I no longer have to go to Kristy's, my head clears like the midday fog off the Golden Gate Bridge, revealing a beauty of a bluesky day, and I have a burst of energy as my hangover vacates the premises.

I straighten and organize my room slowly, reconstructing my deconstructed self by bringing order to the chaos that is my room.

When I'm done I fondle my cash stash like a long-lost lover. Maybe I should ask Sunny if he wants to go in together, get a nice place, start a serious business where we can make the Really Big Money, have a nice room of my own, fix it up, help get Jade out of the junk jungle, and be one big happy family.

I can see it so clearly.

18

EASTER BASKET BONNET

&

HONEY BUNNY

When you prostitute yourself, you have to get paid for it. — Marlena Dietrich

MOTORBIKING THROUGH a sweet Easter Sunday zephyr, I revel in the peaceful afternoon. Or maybe it's me that's peaceful.

As I toodle down Hollywood Boulevard, I can practically hear the Beach Boys singing about all the funfunfun we're gonna have til our Daddy takes the T-Bird away, while the stragglers push their grocerybaskets full of everything they own, like they're hunting for eggs, talking to their own Harvey Easter Bunny.

"Hooo-ie boy, Ah knew you couldn't stay away! Cum on over here an' give Sunny a lil sugah."

Sunny's decked out in a green sparkly dress with dangly bangles and huge fake hooters, and a giant Easter bonnet with an egg-filled Easter basket actually on it.

"Don't I look good enough to eat?" Sunny hoots and hollers. "Did I say that? Hoooooo-ie, I am a bad man!"

You can't help but laugh. So I laugh. And with that the yoke of my load lifts, light as a fig leaf dancing off Adam's junk. I'm home with my homies, celebrated for my winning personality, lack of boundaries, and nuthugging elephantbells.

Sunny motherhen pecks me on both cheeks. I lowfive Godzilla, kiss Cruella, and case the joint. Redheads, deadheads, blondies, brownies, blackies, lackies, hot fudge and cherries, fatties and thinnies, and lots of old faces on young bodies.

Sunny's joint is jive-jumpin' buzz-humpin' packed to the gills, tits to the wind and balls to the wall, as I stride in like a samurai chicken getting bumps from my freaks and my peeps, pecks from my chickens and my chickadees.

I don't see Kristy's pissed-off, shamed humiliation. I don't see her kicking herself for picking me. I don't see her explaining why I stood her up, while her parents shake their disappointed, disapproving heads. I don't see any of that.

I'm looking to get me some Jade.

"Is she here?" I say, way too eager.

"Hold your water, boy. You gotta eat foist." Sunny yanks me towards the kitchen and fixes me a plate of sweet potatoes, black-eyed peas, biscuits, and a couple slabs of ham, pink pig wafting succulent up into my bottomless pit.

When all the food is gone from my plate, Sunny dragqueens me into the livingroom, through the messy mass of Easter madness. On the couch sits a girl in a onepiece bathing suit, fluffy bunny tail, and big floppy ears attached to a barrette clinging hard to her head. She carries an Easter basket full of little airline liquor bottles; marijuana cigarettes; yellow red green blue and teal pills; a sheet with little Mickey Mouses smiling LSDishly from it; and some grey magic mushrooms. The girl is kinda funny looking, but cute, Italian skin, crazy curly brown hair, a goofy off-center nose, chipmunk cheeks, extrathick milkshake lips, eyes the color of a putting green, and an overflowing cornucopia of decolletage.

"This here is Honey Bunny." Sunny nods to me, then winks and leans in to intimate to her: "This here's the boy I'ze telling you about. You do everything he says, and Ah mean evva-ree-thing." He bugs his eyes and she giggles, which makes her jiggle like a bowlful of royal sex jelly.

"Hi, Honey Bunny," I smile, as Sunny spangles away.

"Happy Easter," she replies, like a silly little kid playing dressup.

"I'm always confused about Easter. Is that where Jesus comes back from the dead, peeks his head up from a hole in the ground, and if he sees his shadow, he knows winter's over?" I go right to the A material.

"That's funny . . .did you just make that up?" she stares at me hard and smiles soft. Now she looks like she's a student in an accelerated learning class at Lyndon Baines Johnson High School.

"No, actually, I have a staff of writers working round the clock just churning the shit out." After my deadpan I sneak in a little smile to let her know I'm funning her.

She laughs smart, intelligence burning in her eyes. Comedy is what separates us from the beasts. How did a girl like her end up an Easter Bunny toting intoxicating eggs in Sunny's web? We shall have to get to the bottom of this bunny tale.

Slamming a small Jack I scan the room, surveying the 3D grid for Jade. Where oh where can my baby be? She's at her mom and dad's house on Easter with her dog Marty, trying not to think about what a piece of shit I am.

Change that record, boy.

✗ ✗ ✗

BAD. THAT'S what I am. I'm fifteen and I have done something very bad. I can't now remember what it was, but it was bad. My father grips the steering wheel of the van, his gnarly knuckles snow-white, jaw sprung shut like a bear trap.

"Dad, I'm sorry . . .

"I'm sorry, Dad . . .

"Are you mad, Dad?

"Dad, are you mad?

"Are you mad, Dad?

"Dad, are you mad?

"I'm sorry, Dad . . ."

I want to quit whining, but the more Silence he unleashes on me, the more I become a miserable little stain on the passenger seat.

X   X   X

IT'S SO easy at Sunny's to change any record. There's so much interesting music here.

"So," I smile smooth, "Tell me about yourself."

That's all it takes to get Honey Bunny to spill her guts.

"Well, uh my mom, she died an' my dad, well . . . Dad's a drinker and he used to . . . (lowers her voice) do things . . . (back to normal) to me and Beth, she's my sister, so, uhm, we told our teacher, and my Dad, he got in alotta trouble, I mean . . . alotta trouble, then they sent us to Mercy House, but the counselors there were not very nice, so we told the supervisors, and they calls us a liar, can you believe it? And then things got alot worse, and I mean alot worse, so, uh . . . then we came here and we met Sunny, you know . . . and me and Beth, she's my sister, we got in a big fight, a BIG fight, about Sunny, and um . . . you know, doin' this kinda work . . . and Beth, she ran away, and . . . I'm so worried about her, you know, she could be . . . anywhere, God knows. I hear it's not so bad, being a, uh . . . I mean doin' this kinda work . . . it sure beats flippin' burgers, which I can't even do cuz I'm underage, so, you know, whattaya gonna do? So I decided I'm gonna go to Harvard . . . gonna be a lawyer . . . yeah, I'm gonna go after guys who, you know . . . (lowers her voice) do things . . . (back to normal) to girls, cuz I just don't think that's right, I really don't, it's just not right. It's not that horrible, is it? bein' a . . . you know, doin' this kinda work?"

She looks at me with the big wet eyes of a hungry motherless pup. "It's not that horrible, is it, being a . . . you know, doing this stuff?"

"Better than a sharp stick in the eye," I smile. I tell her to get a specialty, save her money, then get the hell out.

"That's what I'm doing," I hear myself say.

Is that what I'm doing?

Then why am I here instead of at Kristy's parents?

"Thanks." She takes my hand and kisses it, like we're in some medieval fairy tale, and she just made me into a Prince. Suddenly I'm warm toasty tasty with the possibilities of this bundle of desperate, budding, vulnerable, Honey Bunny sexuality.

X X X

HOME ALONE, thirteen, I've recently discovered how much fun it is sliding my hand up and down my penis. Gwenyvere bounds into my room. She's English, adorably happy and sweet, complete with big, beautiful, lovey eyes.

Suddenly she's using me as her human lollipop, and before you can say, lickety split, my lollapalooza is cabooming all over the place.

Gwenyvere seems to really enjoy it.

Frankly, so do I.

I never had a sense of sexual right and wrong.

As far as I'm concerned, we are just a boy and a dog enjoying each other's company.

X X X

HONEY BUNNY looks more delicious by the instant.

"So," I ask, "What's your real name?"

Normally I don't want to know what their real name is. But I like her. She's warm and smart and cuddly and funny and sexy, and it would be such fun to bury myself into her. And I bet she could make a lot of money. Maybe we can find her sister and get her working too, get a nice place together the three of us, get some dogs and cats.

"Sophie," says Honey Bunny.

She looks exactly like a Sophie. I want to protect this girl. And destroy her. Just like I'm doing to myself. Just like I'm doing to Kristy.

I'm about to pop the, "Why don't we go back to my groovy clean pad" question to Sophie, when who should come waltzing in?

Sophie's sister, looking like she's being followed by somebody who likes to "do things" to girls.

Sophie shrieks so loud the party comes to a full stop. She and her sister grab each other like the world's about to come to an end and this is the last thing they want to be doing before the apocalypse.

After the assembled let out a collective sigh, roll their eyes, and make their catty remarks, the party comes back to life, and I watch the little sister be swallowed up in the big sister.

Sophie strips off her bunny accoutrements, and the sisters whisper with each other. Little sister's in dirty white overalls, longer and leaner than Sophie, but clearly from the same gene pool.

Hey, maybe I can have sex with both of them. Maybe the gods are smiling on me after all.

Sophie looks like a big sister now, so sweet and easy and full of comfort. I see me and my little brother the night of the Great Pea Scandal of '64, just the two of us in our beds, me and my little brother, who'll always love each other no matter what. I miss him so much.

Sophie drags Little Sister over to meet me.

"OH MY GOD! I can't believe it, I cannot believe it, uh, this is Beth, my sister, I was telling you about . . . So, uh . . . you're not gonna believe this, but uh, Beth, she called our cousin Roger, he's in Phoenix, and he said we can, uh, come and stay with him until we figure out what we're gonna, uh . . . do, this is unbelievable, don't you think it's unbelievable? I just think it's . . . unbelievable . . . don't you?"

I have a vision of Sophie and Beth telling their kids and their grandkids about that day they escaped in just the nick of time.

19

THE WALRUS

&

THE SCALPING OF JULIETTE

I am not a slut, though I thank the gods I am foul. — Shakespeare

X X X

THE LAST day I am a chicken. The phone rings.

"Hey, boy." There's no *et toi* in Sunny's voice.

"What's the matter?" My ass starts to hurt.

"Got some bad news. Call jest come in. Jade . . . she's dead. Last night. Ah'm sorry, Ah know you had a thing for her, so Ah wanted you to hear it from me," Sunny says soft.

My heart sinks with me as I collapse onto the couch. I see Jade dancing to that tune playing in her head, half geisha half trained killer. Big tears suddenly fill my eyes and I cover my face with my hands to stop them from coming out. They're so close, right there, waiting. But I won't let them out. I don't understand how tears work yet.

"You aw-ite, boy?"

Sunny brings me back to the land of the living.

"You sure you wanna woik tonight? Ya wanna cancel?" Sunny shifts seamlessly from concerned family member to calculating business manager.

I shut it down, pack it up, and store it away.

"No, I'm cool. It's sad, but like you said, she was a messed-up girl. Hey, five hundred bucks is five hundred bucks, right?"

"Yeah aw–ite, well . . . come by when you done."

And then Sunny is gone.

Jade was probably junked up, did something stupid, got herself whacked or jacked or smacked.

Not my fault. Not my problem.

Whatever.

X X X

JULIETTE IS French and very refined, by far the most functional member of our family unit. In the back yard my father calls Juliette, and she bounds over happily, ready to love and be loved.

As she gets to the picnic table, she makes eye contact with my dad, and her tail snaps up hard between her legs, everything shrinking up as she tries to slink away unnoticed.

But there's no escape for Juliette.

My dad grabs her, one hand on the collar, one under the belly, plops her down on the picnic table covered with a stained sheet, fires up the old sheep shearer, and begins scalping the defenseless Juliette, who looks around with the biggest, saddest, how–much–is–that–doggy–in–the–window eyes, like some captured French freedom fighter pleading, "'elp me, s'il vous plait!"

We can't help ourselves, how can we help her?

My old man shaves and shaves the whimpering Juliette until there's five pounds of curly black pubes on the old stained sheet, and she's barebuttbald.

Juliette spends the next weeks hiding under tables, chairs, and beds, ashamed to face the humiliating heckling of the neighborhood dogs.

I'll soon know how she feels.

✗ ✗ ✗

OLD, STUFFY, puffing a pipe with a mustache, he looks like a walrus in a blood-red smoking jacket. He wears no slippers, and his long narrow feet are covered by skin so translucent you can see pale blue rivers running under it. He sits too erect, trying to suck in his gut, like he's posing for a portrait with an invisible javelin stuck up his ass. His pad's neat as a pin with a cleaning disorder, and lavishly appointed with rich rugs, gaudy goblets, and kitschy knick-knacks. A scratchy 78 of Judy Garland doing "Happiness Is a Thing Called Joe" plays on an old-time Victrola. He looks like he's constructed his life so he's the star of his own Noel Coward play.

I can't wait to wipe that thin grin off his smug mug.

No instructions have been given. He did hand me five hundred dollars, but when I took it he held on to it too long, so I had to yank it out of his hand. That made me mad. I gotta tell Sunny. From now on, I want an envelope, on the table, no questions asked.

I'm gunslinger calm, but my blood bubbles bubbles toil and troubles, and a brainfever so severe I can barely see straight rages up inside me.

I'm focusing my beam right at this old rich stuckup queen and his walrus mustache.

✗ ✗ ✗

THE SCALPING of Juliette is now a week behind us, and it's the night before our family's going on vacation. My dad lines us all up: me, my brother, and my cousins, while Juliette sneaks furtive glances from around the corner, reliving her horror, wondering if she'll be next.

My father grabs my nine-year-old head with one hand, thumb and forefinger squeezing temples, the sheepshearer buzz surround-sounding me, loud and louder, scraping like nails across the blackboard of my

jangling nerves, 'til I'm vibrating with the exact same frequency, as my
dad buzzcuts his way across the quivering egg of my head.

X X X

BULLET HOLE in Jade's forehead flashes so clear on the inside of my eyes—

Change the record.

I look around the Walrus's room for some lifejacket to jack into, and I
spot a cheesy figurine of Peter Pan, all in green, head to toe, with those
pointy little green shoes, and that Puck grin.

Tinkerbell. Is she dead, too?

Change the record.

The Walrus drones in a nasal monotone about how he saw me at the
orgy, and how he knew he had to have me. Have me? A wolverine snarl
curls inside me. I think you're confused. It's me who's gonna have you.

He wants to know if I remember him from the orgy. He was dressed as
a satyr, the mythological half-man half-beast who embodies raw sexuality
and is hung like a horse.

He wants me to remember him. So I pretend I remember him. Tell
him what a great costume he had, how I believe we've lost sight of our
animal selves as we get more civilized, and that I wasn't surprised he was
hung like a horse.

He likes it. Which is why I say it. But it's getting warm in here. This
trick seems to be under the mistaken impression that some kind of sex is
about to happen here. We'll have to disabuse him of that notion quickly.
And he's always playing with that mustache. Twirling it, stroking it, mas-
saging it. Makes me want to slap it right off his face, and watch the red
rose of a bruise bloom on his cheek.

Almost like he's reading my mind, he shoots me a look like he thinks
he's a real naughty boy. I shoot him back some cold hard steel.

Let the games begin.

X X X

HEAVYMETAL SHEEP shearer scalds my skull. I smell the warm oily machineness, and I hear my hairs scream out as they're shorn short, shocked, trickling prickly and itchy, shivering down my back.

As my dad mows the yard of my head, the grip of his vice tightens around my temples, and I absorb it into me like a new computer with an empty hard drive, his fingers plugged into the USB ports on either side of my head, filling me with an angry silent virus.

And then we're barebuttbald, just like Juliette.

Everyone's extra quiet at bedtime, none of the jocularity and staying-up-late behavior that characterizes our group dynamic, no teasing about how ugly we look, cuz we all look ugly, little Samsons sapped of our strength.

X X X

THE WALRUS wants me to come over to him. I still don't know what he wants. I don't like that. I don't like him.

Jade impaled on a junkspike.

I want to plant my fist in the garden of his face. I walk over to him hard with my fist closed tight, and I move to smack him, just a little move, but full of all the violence that's hiding under my kitchen table.

He cringes and gets hard at the same time.

"Wait a second, sonny, I've gotta get . . . in the mood," the Walrus whinges.

I ain't your sonny, and I don't give a damn about your mood. I'm ready to smack you around and get the hell out.

The Walrus slowly opens up his smoking jacket, with an "aren't I a naughty boy?" look.

Under his smoking blood-colored jacket is a black leather bustier with a bulletbra.

The Walrus doesn't look like a naughty boy to me. He seems like somebody I want to watch double up in agony. But he wants me to tell him what a naughty boy he is, I know that, so I swallow myself again and add another bone to the cauldron bubbling inside me.

"Wow," I say, "that is some crazy shit."

He pats a spot on the loveseat. He wants me to sit down next to him. On the loveseat.

DO NOT SIT ON THE LOVESEAT!

My brain screams at me as I sit on the loveseat, while a thin line of sweat heads south from under my arm.

"Hey, man, let's get one thing straight here. We're not doing any . . . sex thing here, you understand that, right?"

He smiles like a community theater player trying to portray a suave cad/manabouttown, and the sheer smarm of him almost knocks me off the chair.

"Yes, I guess we need to get it . . . 'straight' "— he's thrilled with himself for being so damn witty— "No, I have a wonderful itinerary planned for us, but you will not be required to do any . . ."

The mocking nags at my guts. He thinks he's smarter than me. He thinks he's better than me. Not for long, my friend.

". . . sex things . . ." The Walrus leers like a loungelizard in a bulletbra.

He puts his hand on my head, which makes my stomach jump, and shrivels my balls. He pulls my head toward him and rests it on the cold leather of the chest of the bullet bra.

The thin sheet of ice is cracking all around me.

✗ ✗ ✗

BAREBUTTBALD I finally arrive excited on the Florida shore for our family vacation. We spend our first day cavorting on the beach under the torrent of tropical sun. I keep feeling like my head's too hot. I try to tell a grownup, but I'm shushed. That night, all the boys complain about how hot their heads are.

Sunpoisoning of the scalp. That's what we got. Painful puffing pussing and peeling follow. Worst of all, we have to wear these dumbass floppy golf hats like doddering codgers.

After that I have a special relationship with Juliette. She shoots me meaningful glances from time to time. I nod knowingly. We're members of the Barebuttbald club.

✗ ✗ ✗

LEATHER SMELL fills me as it wafts up from the bulletbra'd bustier. The Walrus is pressing my head into it.

I can see out of my eye corner that the Walrus is manipulating himself under his silky pajama bottom, and I vibrate with his nasty, spastic jerky jerkoff rhythm.

Change the record.

Jade's dead empty eyes—

There is a rhythmic tug on my head as my long hair hangs in my face, prickly on my cheek.

I hear a sickly sucking sound that matches the rhythmic tugs on my head. I strain to see what's making that sucking sound on my skull.

At the extreme corner of my sightline I spot the Walrus's face, tilted back, eyes rolled up so only the runny-egg whites are showing.

The Walrus has my hair in his mouth.

The Walrus is sucking on my hair.

Something all the way inside of me pops, I rocket to my feet, my hair clumped and wet with Walrus spittle.

"What the hell is wrong with you, asshole?!" I roar like a prehistoric monster.

"Now, wait a minute! I'm not—"

"No, you wait a minute, bitch!"

I slap him across the cheek.

WHACK! Loud. Skin on skin. That's good.

"Please!"

Worry wades across the face of the Walrus as he pleads and bleeds from the corner of his mouth. At this moment he realizes he's made a dangerous mistake inviting me into his parlor to play his little reindeer games.

The scare coming out of him makes me high.

"Shut up, punk!"

I pick up his Cowardly Lion statuette and throw it as hard as I can against the wall, where it shatters into a galaxy of tiny little scared lion pieces. Then I throw a fancy painted-rock egg thing through his glass cabinet. He screams, and I reward him with a knuckled backhanded rap upside his head, which whips backwards as he's jettisoned off the loveseat to the plushy rug, while I feel more alive than I have in a long time. This one's for Jade, bastard! I rear my foot back and let fly, making solid contact with his stomach, his guts rocking backwards as his breath disappears. The Walrus shakes on the floor, wheezing, fetal, looking up at me with a silent plea for sanity.

I pick up a Mae West–shaped lamp with two bulbs for breasts and fling it into a mirror, tit bulbs and shiny shattered platinum hair shooting everywhere.

There's a long lamp by a chair, six feet and skinny, with a heavy metal bottom base. I raise it high and it's heavy, perfectly weighted, the ideal tool for the job of cracking this Walrus like a coconut and watching the brainmilk drain out. I stalk towards him, fury blasting out of me like a fire-and-brimstone preacher.

The Walrus has wet his silk pajamas. I feel kind of bad for the guy. He just wanted a little slap and tickle. Not this hurricane of pain.

But I can't stop myself.

I bring that metalheaded pole flinging down with all my might, but instead of Walrus head I smash glass table, shards shooting and spitting.

TV. Yes. Next I swing that lampclub like it's a Big Bertha and I'm bombing the screen straight down the fairway. Smoke and sparks zip around like an electrical storm in a lighted globe.

I'm hot sweaty and breathy, having violence orgasms as I shatter my way through the Walrus's life.

I stalk back over to the Walrus, who's muttering.

"Please, please, please . . ."

"Wanna suck on my hair again, you piece of shit?" The hate flows from me as I dance with the devil's snake, leading hordes of Huns over the horizon to splay women and eat children.

Jade gagged with a plastic bag over her head.

I reach down slow, grab his rug, rip it off his head, and shove it into his mouth.

"How's that taste? Isn't that sexy?"

Then I rear back and punch him right in the nose. I always wanted to do that. You see it so much in the movies and it looks so cool. But in real life it's not nearly that good. Hurts the hell out of my knuckles. It does make a nice sound, though, that thwack of bone hard on bone.

Walrus head drives back into the wall behind it with a thick thud.

I stormtrooper around his pad, smashing thrashing and trashing, jazzed with madness.

I squat on my haunches, and lean down like his face is the camera and I'm going in for my extreme close-up.

"If you tell Sunny or anybody else about this I'm gonna come back and finish you off, you understand me?"

No response.

The Walrus isn't moving. I shake him. Nothing.

"Hey, you all right?"

No response.

Now I'm scared. He's just laying there. I see crime scene photos of the fallen Walrus, his pristine apartment looking like Dresden after the bombing. Oh shit what have I done? I put my hand in front of his mouth. The Walrus is still breathing. He is definitely still breathing.

Walking away as fast as I can, I raise my defense shields to stop the raw rank fear that's trying to pin me on the bed and slam its way inside me.

✗ ✗ ✗

PLAYING BALL with the older neighborhood boys when I am five. Somebody throws the ball over my head and it rolls into the yard next door, where there's an old mean German shepherd who's been chained to a pole for about a hundred years.

White ball sits in green grass. When I crawl through the opening in the fence, and reach down to grab the ball, I hear a metallic snap of a chain breaking. I look up and the German shepherd is flying at me, giant teeth bared, hungry for my flesh. I move at the last second, and the dog's mouth chomps onto my thigh, inches from my little penis.

I scream, and the whole neighborhood comes rushing.

✗ ✗ ✗

SPEEDWALKING TO my motorbike, fingering busted-up pager and knuckle-hurts like hell. I see cops swarming the Walrus pad with dogs, dusting for fingerprints, scouring every inch of the place for proof that it was me. Front page of the *LA Times* with a big picture of me being dragged away in handcuffs, BOY HOOKER BUSTED. My mom and dad in court, disgraced, my head bowed in shame, condemned by the Judge I abused as a symbol of everything that's wrong with America. Kristy and her parents in the back shaking their head. Waking up in prison with a tall SEXY man all up in me.

Change the record nownownow!

A plan. I need a plan. I could keep driving until I get to an Indian reservation and live there. Go to Alaska and work on the pipeline. Lots of good work for a handy guy on the pipeline. Go to Mexico. Got enough money to live like a king on the beach, get a senorita who cooks my meals and loves me.

I drive past my street but I don't go down it. Hordes of feds and G-men are probably going through my stuff, searching for the piece of evidence that's gonna send me to the stripey hole where I shall suffer the rest of my days.

Oh shit, what's Sunny gonna think? I've been avoiding this thought, but now it bores full force into me. To hell with that bastard pimp. I'll turn him in. Hey, if I'm going down, I'm taking everybody down with me. What am I thinking? Those Hollywood Employment Agency bastards are killers. They will seriously kill you.

Hold everything. In my rear view mirror is a cop. He's giving me the hardcore five-oh eyeball. Or am I just feeling the eyeball? No idea. I turn down Vine. He follows me. Oh shit. I come within a whisper on a whisker of gunning it, and leading him on a high-speed chase away from the LAPD on the six o'clock news.

But I stick steady, turn off onto a side street, take another fast turn, and lose him. I say lose, but I guess technically you can't lose somebody who's not actually following you.

A plan, a plan, I need a plan.

I have a mystic vision.

Kristy.

I'll come clean. I'll make it up to her. I will force her to love me.

The pager is hard cold and black in my pocket.

I can see clearly now that this is the source of Evil in my life. I slam on my brakes. Hop off my bike. Take the pager from my pocket. Slowly I raise it over my head.

The pager is hard cold and black in my hand as a righteous rush floods me and I slam my arm down as fast as I can.

SMASH!

The pager hits the pavement and bursts into a million cold, hard black pieces, flying everywhere. Staring at the guts of my pager spread out all over the stars on Hollywood Boulevard, I feel like a hero who's just slain the evil ogre monster.

Free at last. Free at last. Free at last.

I am a chicken no more.

20

I WANNA HAVE SEX

When the end comes I know they'll say just a gigolo,
life goes on without me — L. Casucci/I. Cesar–S. Willams/R. Graham

MY BUSTED up knuckle hurts like hell, but I have no pager to finger as I park my bike and pull it up onto its stand quiet. It's dark and I'm animal-aware of every sound on this little Hollywood sidestreet. So this is what it feels like to be on the FBI Ten Most Wanted list. Someone's lurking behind every tree, about to slam around every corner, bounce out of every fake utility truck to bust my shit. Breathe. I wish I had a gun. I wonder where I can get a gun. Sunny'll know. Oh shit, Sunny. He's gonna hate me now. After everything he did for me, I jacked him right where he lives. Hey, he deserves it.

Whatever.

Suddenly a car pulls up fast and parks about twenty feet away, on the same side of the street as me. I duck behind the side of a building. A couple of clean-looking guys get out quick, looking like Hollywood Employment Agency hired goons come to rough me up and down. They're walking toward me. One of them reaches in his coat pocket for a gun. Oh shit. I start to make a mad dash for it when he pulls out his keys. No gun. The only gun is in my head, and it's loaded and cocked, my own finger slowly squeezing the trigger.

Got to get ahold of myself. The Walrus splayed out on the floor. Jade with her throat cut. Do you love Mommy, Braddy? How did this happen to me? No, this didn't happen to me. I made it happen. But I didn't want to leave home. It's not my fault my father's having a nervous breakdown. It's not my fault my mother buggered off with her lover and didn't invite me along. Is that my fault? Hell no.

Whatever.

The Walrus got what was coming to him. If he's smart this asswhupping'll turn his life around and make him a productive member of society. Hell, I did the guy a favor. And besides, who's he gonna tell? The cops? What's he gonna say? That he paid a chicken to rough him up and things got a little out of hand? I don't think so.

I will confess to my girl. I will baptize myself in the holy water of Kristy.

I walk behind the building to her little bungalow. I knock on her door. No answer. I have no Plan B. Maybe I'll just wait here until she comes home. Knock again. No answer. Shit.

I sit down on her stoop, prepared to wait for the rest of my life if necessary. But just as I settle, the door opens.

It's Kristy. God I like this girl.

She doesn't see anyone at her door. She's confused. She wasn't expecting anyone, heard two knocks, and no one is there.

Guilt punches me in the chest. Why did I betray her? Only a terrible person would do something like that. If I'd just done the right thing I wouldn't have pummeled that innocent pervert.

If ifs and ands were pots and pans, beggars would be kings. My mother used to say that.

Kristy feels someone staring at her, looks down, and when she sees it's me, her whole face tightens and darkens and hardens.

A wasp of shame stings me.

xxx

ENDURING THE Sixties as a Hausfrau ensured that my mom would not miss the Seventies doing laundry and cooking for a man who's not really there.

At this time the Women's Movement is rearing its Sapphic head and roaring in all its glory. Consciousnesses are being raised willy-nilly, vaginas examined in mirrors, and bras burned in every city, burb, and village.

Our Bodies, Our Selves makes the rounds in our house. We're all free to be you and me. Mommies are people, people with feelings.

It's all right to cry.

xxx

GLACIAL COLD snaps down from Kristy and chills my blood. She used to look at me so nice.

"What do you want?"

"Please, Kristy, I'm sorry, I really am. I'm so sorry. Just give me five minutes. Please . . ." This is where I, master apologist, must begin.

"No, I don't think so." Kristy is unmoved.

"Please, I'm begging you, just give me five minutes . . . Kristy I'm desperate, please. I'm so sorry . . ." I plunge into fullfrontal grovel.

A huge sad rushes up me, and the tears are there again, only this time I don't stop them. I don't remember crying in front of someone my own age before, but I want back in so bad, I'm willing to walk a trail of tears to get there. My eyes get fuller and fuller, like udders that need to be milked. Then two waterfalls wash down the rock of my face, as I slowly empty.

Something moves in Kristy. She's not ready to let me back, but her good sweet heart is feeling me.

"Kristy, something really terrible happened to me, something I can't tell anybody about. But I want to tell you, so you'll understand. Please, I'm begging you."

"All right, come in," she sighs like she's lending money to someone she knows'll never pay her back. "I'm so mad at you. It was so embarrassing. My mom kept shaking her head the whole time, like I'm ten years old. And not even a phone call. How long does that take? Thirty seconds to make a phone call . . ."

This is good. Honest punishment I deserve. Suddenly I'm not some sick sadochicken, I'm just some dumb shlub who messed up with his girl, like a million dumb shlubs before me. When she's railing on me I can imagine we're a couple in the middle of a spat we'll look back on years from now and laugh about.

"I know, I'm so sorry. See, I meant to tell you this. I'm . . . I was . . . embarrassed. And the truth is . . .

"I'm a . . .

"I've been . . .

". . .selling drugs . . ."

X X X

EDUCATION SUCKS so bad in Dallas that my mom starts the Dallas Free School. One of the teachers is an earnest young educator out of the MIDWEST. Roundfaced, blond, and whipsmart, she takes no guff, but at the same time she's patient and kind, a great teacher and an allaround good egg. My mother and her new best friend start attending teaching conferences, and National Organization of Women's meetings, and Gloria Steinem fundraisers. These women are not quilting, or swapping recipes, or buying Tupperware. They're pissed off. They want equal pay for equal work, alimony payment protection, and day-care reform. They want to stop the war and feed the children. Equality, liberation, and R–E–S–P–E–C–T. They want clitoral orgasms and Freud be damned!

So my mom sings, she marches, she gets naked and feels comfortable with her own beautiful female body in deeply feminine ways no man can ever understand. While my father builds his high-tech state-of-the-art explosives factory in Useless, Texas.

X X X

I GIVE Kristy a song and dance of epic portions, apologies flying thick and fast. But I do want to make it right. That's the truth.

Kristy slowly shakes her disgusted head.

"Why would you do something like that? Why didn't you tell me? How can—"

I cut her off at the pass. I'm not a teenage prostitute anymore, but now I'm a drug dealer, which is not much better; plus it means I've been lying to her, which is bad very very bad. So I launch right into the whole Sunny/dumpster/working at the restaurant/becoming a hooker ordeal (minus SEXY), only I substitute drugs for chickening.

"Like I said, I was embarrassed. I'm really sorry . . . but I like you so much and I felt like such a freak . . ."

Long silence.

I wait for her to tell me to get out. Or call me over for the hug. But she just stands there and looks at me. More silence. I can hear the tumblers rolling around in her head as she tries to fit all this new information into her jigsaw puzzle of me.

"What do you want from me?" she finally says.

"I wanna have sex."

Before I can stop it, somehow that miserable sentence bolts past security and out of my mouth. Even as it's emerging, I want to suck it back in and say something sweet, soft, and cuddly.

The storm that's been brewing in Kristy rages out at me.

"You blow me off, then show up the next night, and you expect me to have sex with you? You are unbelievable."

"I'm sorry, I'm—" sinking so fast.

"I can't do it anymore. You need to go now." Kristy's made up her mind. I can see it in her spine.

"What're you saying? Are you breaking up with me?" I'm not a lover-studguy, I'm a pathetic loser who betrayed his sweet girl.

"Yes, I am. Now I'd like you to leave."

I'm done. I disengage, pull the switch down, and the Silence descending over me.

"Whatever."

This is the last word I ever say to Kristy.

When I leave her house, something turns off inside me. I have no more Kristy. I've ejected myself in a bloody blaze of violence from the chicken industry, so I have no 3D.

Arrest me, shoot me, I don't care anymore.

I am, of course, ravenously hungry. So I get my dayold birthday cake, my ice cream, and my milk, take it home, and shovel it all into my face with doomed fervor. As yet another lactose seizure squats upon me, I see strange lights I've never seen before, at the edge of my eyes. At first I can't tell if the lights are really there, because whenever I look directly at them, they move somewhere else. Then a pain strikes inside my head, like someone's drilling a thin diamond bit into my brain with each breath I take, knocking me down on the bed with nausea.

Then I'm asleep.

Even though I never want to think about them again, my fever dreams that night star Kristy, Sunny, Mommy, The Walrus, but most especially SEXY. They will make cameo guest star appearances in my nightmares and flashbacks for decades, until getting my head cracked open in that crack den leads me to finally exorcising their ghosts in this memoir.

Acknowledgments

I would like to acknowledge my parents for all the love and support they gave me. I thank my brothers and sisters for being sources of love and sweetness, often in the face of enormous idiocy and nastiness on my part. James Levine, president of Levine Greenberg Literary Agency, was not only enormously helpful as a keen, astute, and cunning business advisor, but he was also instrumental in forming the structure of *Chicken*, with several brilliant suggestions. Melissa and Mike must also be metaphorically patted on the back for their contributions. I thank Judith Regan for originally publishing this book, and making some very smart suggestions. Michael Amy Sterry Marcario Cira Shippo must be thanked for being a good and constant friend. Thank you to Steph for being a good friend for many years, and to Ruth and Sam for being Ruth and Sam. Judy deserves special kudos for being so patient and understanding. Larry Jones lent me $500 when I needed it, and he's been making me laugh and think for a long time. Alex Kenny taught me everything I know.

Katie Humes was very helpful in reading and giving comments and being generally kind and wonderful. Susan Wooldridge was immensely helpful technically, spiritually, and emotionally. Louis Stein must be noted for his extraordinary contributions in the areas of humor, goodwill, and general excellence. Jack Haley and Laura Sedlock were kind enough to give me very useful advice. Susie Greeneboom let me spread like a virus in her apartment as I wrote this. Iggy and Pascal Breninkmeyer, Irene, and Kylie were kind enough to let me sleep on their couch.

Tina Jacobsen must be singled out twice. Once, for being a brilliant agent who took a lump of coal and crafted a diamond out of it. Then for being a brilliant friend who gave my insane manuscript to her goddaughter, the agent. Thank you Tina. You are a rare and lovely human being.

Which brings us to the mother lode. The goddaughter of Tina. The one and only Snow Leopard herself, the apple in my coffee, the cream in my eye: Arielle Eckstut. Besides being the greatest agent I ever had by leaps and bounds (and I've had more agents than any human should), and having the insight and guts to help me tell the truth, she is also a gorgeous beauty, a great friend to cats even though she's allergic to them, a wild animal, a deep thinker, a profound wit, the best of friends, an excellent driver, a wonderful writer, an expert Austenian, a hot chick, a world-class mother, and a sweet and loving human of the highest order. Even living to be 120 years old, I will never be able to thank her enough.